Gabriel García Márquez

Twayne's World Authors Series

Latin American Literature

David Foster, Editor
Arizona State University

TWAS 749

Gabriel García Márquez, 1981
Photograph courtesy of Wide World Photos

Gabriel García Márquez

By Raymond L. Williams

Washington University, St. Louis

Twayne Publishers • Boston

Gabriel García Márquez

Raymond L. Williams

Copyright © 1984 by G. K. Hall & Company
All Rights Reserved
Published by Twayne Publishers
A Division of G. K. Hall & Company
70 Lincoln Street
Boston, Massachusetts 02111

Book Production by Elizabeth Todesco

Book Design by Barbara Anderson

Printed on permanent/durable acid-free
paper and bound in the United States of
America.

Library of Congress Cataloging in Publication Data

Williams, Raymond L.
  Gabriel García Márquez.

  (Twayne's world authors series; TWAS 749. Latin
American literature)
  Bibliography: p. 166
  Includes index.
  1. García Márquez, Gabriel, 1928–
—Criticism and interpretation.
  I. Title.   II. Series: Twayne's world authors series: TWAS 749.
III. Series: Twayne's world authors series. Latin American literature.
PQ8180.17.A73Z95 1984   863   84–6754
ISBN 0–8057–6597–2
ISBN 0–8057–6615–4 (Pbk)

For Germán, Susie, Mauricio, and la cachaca

Contents

About the Author

Raymond L. Williams is associate professor of Spanish at Washington University in St. Louis. He received his B.A. (with Highest Honors) from Washington State University in 1972, and the M.A. (1974) and Ph.D. (1977) from the University of Kansas. He was a Fulbright Scholar in Colombia in 1975–76, and has taught at the University of Chicago.

He is the author of *Una década de la novela colombiana: la experiencia de los setenta* (1981) and three other books. His articles have been published in both U.S. academic journals and foreign magazines, including *Hispania, Symposium, Kentucky Romance Quarterly, Revista de estudios hispánicos, Revista iberoamericana, Hispanorama, Texas Studies in Language and Literature, El café literario, Explicación de textos literarios,* and *Texto crítico.*

Preface

The Spanish-American novel burst into prominence in the 1960s for readers outside the Spanish-speaking world. Gabriel García Márquez has been among the most celebrated of these Latin American writers, especially since receiving the Nobel Prize for Literature in 1982. This book intends to provide a general introduction and overview of his entire writing career and analyses of his complete fiction. It is directed to both the student or layman perhaps recently initiated into the wonders of Macondo—García Márquez's fictional world—and the teacher or scholar well acquainted with his work and the critical literature devoted to it.

In accordance with the format of many studies in this series, I begin with a brief biographical introduction (chapter 1), and then discuss the individual works in a basically chronological fashion. I might add that such a format is particularly useful in the case of García Márquez because a chronological understanding of his complete work can radically change one's conception of any single text read in isolation. *One Hundred Years of Solitude,* for example, is a much different novel once read with a knowledge of previous works, such as *Leafstorm* or *In Evil Hour.*

Several of the finest scholars of Latin American literature have already studied García Márquez extensively. A complete list of even the books, not to mention the enormous body of articles, would be too lengthy to enumerate and discuss here. John S. Brushwood's *The Spanish American Novel: A Twentieth Century Survey* places García Márquez within the context of Spanish-American fiction in general and offers perceptive analyses of individual novels in succinct and jargon-free language. Book-length studies by George McMurray and Regina Janes provide sound readings and often penetrating commentary on specific texts. Readers of Spanish will find Mario Vargas Llosa's *Gabriel García Márquez: historia de un deicidio* most illuminating. Two of this Peruvian novelist's strongest points are his personal acquaintance with García Márquez and his understanding of Latin American society. The present study differs from the above in many ways, but most importantly in the emphasis and information it offers concerning the early period of García Márquez's career, the readings and approaches to individual texts, and the fact that it includes more of García Márquez's total fiction than the above-mentioned books, including much of the journalism.

Several technical matters invite comment. First, the passages translated in this book are mostly from the published English editions. The non-Spanish reader will be pleased to know that Gregory Rabassa, García Márquez's translator, provides the reader with an English text impressively similar to the original. In short, he is a superb translator. If no reference to a translation appears in the text, it is mine. Second, when referring to a novel or story several times, I have used a note citation only in the first instance. After that, page references appear parenthetically within the text. Third, I would offer a few clarifications concerning the use of Spanish and English texts. Since all of García Márquez's novels are known to readers in the United States by their English titles, I refer to them with these titles. The dates of publication in both the Chronology and the body of this study, however, refer to the original publication date in the Spanish.

For the general readership to whom this book is directed, a conscientious effort has been made to avoid technical language. When a specifically limited set of terms with special meanings is used, these terms are explained in each chapter and footnoted. Four terms appear with regularity. The first, *la violencia,* refers to that historical period in Colombia of civil war between Liberals and Conservatives usually dated from approximately 1948 to 1958. The second is Walter Ong's term, "fictionalized reader." Ong points out that just as an author invents characters, he invents readers. One important factor in any author's success, then, is his ability to fictionalize a reader whose role the real reader desires or is willing to play. The third term, "heteroglossia," is perhaps best understood by thinking first of the Greek roots, "hetero," meaning "other," and "glossia," meaning "languages." M. Bakhtin has popularized this term, referring to the "other languages" or a variety of different languages which literary texts often incorporate. For example, a writer may incorporate the language of another writer, or the language of such spheres as politics or religion. The last term which I occasionally use is "ideologeme," a word which refers to a socially symbolic act, according to Fredric Jameson. The discourses of different social classes, of course, vary; an ideologeme is the smallest intelligible unit of the essentially antagonistic collective discourses of social classes.

A matter of some importance is my own foreignness. It is sometimes difficult working in a foreign literature to see the material with the sense of cultural identification that is natural in dealing with one's native literature. I hope that my extended residence in Colombia, regular visits there, and research on Colombian writers will serve as a reasonable compensation. My efforts have been supported by the Fulbright Commission of Colombia and by both the Graduate School and the Department of Romance Languages at Washington University.

I would like to acknowledge with gratitude those persons who helped in different ways, such as suggesting readings or making valuable suggestions concerning the manuscript: John S. Brushwood, Michael Doudoroff, David W. Foster, James F. Jones, William Kirby, Harvey Oberhelman, Frances Stadler, and Germán Vargas. A special thanks to my research assistant, Stephanie Hedstrom, and my typist, Debra Jones. The project would have been enormously more difficult without the assistance and support of my wife, Pamela. The final product, however, is mine, as are its inevitable errors or inaccuracies.

Raymond L. Williams

Washington University, St. Louis

Chronology

1928 Gabriel García Márquez born in Aracataca, a small town near the Caribbean coast of Colombia.

1946 Completes high school education, Bogotá.

1947 Publishes first story, "La tercera resignación" ("The Third Resignation"), in a newspaper.
Begins law studies, Universidad Nacional, Bogotá.

1948 Presidential candidate Jorge Eliécer Gaitán is assassinated. García Márquez moves from Bogotá to Cartagena on the coast, and continues studies of law and writes journalism.

1950 Discontinues law studies and joins staff of the newspaper *El Heraldo* in Barranquilla, where he writes a regular column. Continues publishing short stories.

1954 Returns to Bogotá; writes for the newspaper *El Espectador.*

1955 Publishes his first novel, *La hojarasca (Leafstorm).* Wins national prize for a short story. Goes to Geneva as correspondent for *El Espectador.* The newspaper is closed by the government; by the end of the year he is living in Paris and writing fiction.

1956 Lives in Paris, unemployed, and works on manuscripts for two novels: *La mala hora (In Evil Hour)* and *El coronel no tiene quien le escriba (No One Writes to the Colonel).*

1957 Finishes the manuscript for *No One Writes to the Colonel.* Travels throughout Eastern Europe.

1958 Arrives in Caracas. Marries Mercedes Barcha. Works for the newspaper *El Momento* in Caracas. Writes almost all the stories that will later be published in the volume *Los funerales de la Mamá Grande* [Big mama's funeral].

1959 Cuban Revolution. Works for Cuba's Prensa Latina in Bogotá, Cuba, and New York.

1961 Publishes *No One Writes to the Colonel.* Awarded National Novel Prize in Colombia for *In Evil Hour.* Makes "homage to Faulkner" bus trip through the Deep South to Mexico City.

1962 Publishes *In Evil Hour* and *Big Mama's Funeral.*

1965 Goes into seclusion to begin writing *Cien años de soledad (One Hundred Years of Solitude).*

1967 *One Hundred Years of Solitude* published in Buenos Aires.

1969 *One Hundred Years of Solitude* receives Chianchiano Prize in Italy.

1970 First edition in English of *One Hundred Years of Solitude. Time* magazine names it one of twelve best books of the year.

1971 The Peruvian novelist and critic Mario Vargas Llosa publishes an extensive study on the complete work of García Márquez: *Gabriel García Márquez: historia de un deicidio* (Gabriel García Márquez: history of a deicide).

1972 Receives the Rómulo Gallegos Prize. Publishes *La increíble y triste historia de la cándida Eréndira y de su abuela desalmada (The Incredible and Sad Tale of Innocent Eréndira and Her Heartless Grandmother). Books Abroad* awards him the Neustadt Prize.

1973 Publishes *Cuando era feliz e indocumentado* (When I was happy and undocumented), a compilation of journalism from the late 1950s.

1974 Founds *Alternativa,* a leftist magazine, in Bogotá.

1975 Publishes *El otoño del patriarca (The Autumn of the Patriarch).*

1977 Publishes *Operación Carlota* (Operation Carlota), an essay on Cuba's role in Africa.

1981 Publishes *Crónica de una muerte anunciada (Chronicle of a Death Foretold).*

1982 Awarded Nobel Prize for Literature. Publishes *El olor de la guayaba* (The Fragrance of Guava), conversations with Plinio Apuleyo Mendoza.

Chapter One
Introduction and Biography
The Phenomenon of Gabriel García Márquez

"In about the middle of 1967, the novel *One Hundred Years of Solitude* was published in Buenos Aires, provoking a literary earthquake throughout Latin America. The critics recognized the book as a masterpiece of the art of fiction and the public endorsed this opinion, systematically exhausting new editions, which, at one point, appeared at the astounding rate of one a week. Overnight, García Márquez became almost as famous as a great player or an eminent singer of boleros."[1] Thus the eminent Latin American novelist Mario Vargas Llosa wrote of the astonishing impact of *One Hundred Years of Solitude* in the Hispanic world. Vargas Llosa would soon become so fascinated with García Márquez's work that he would dedicate a monumental 667-page book to the study of García Márquez's total fiction. It was, however, not only the Hispanic world that was stunned, perplexed, or fascinated by *One Hundred Years of Solitude*. As translations began to appear, the accolades were immediate and profuse throughout the world: *One Hundred Years of Solitude* received the Chianchiano Prize in Italy (1969); the French named it the best foreign book of the year (1969); American critics chose it as one of the best books of the year (1970). During the 1970s other honors were bestowed on García Márquez, such as *Books Abroad*'s Neustadt Award, the Rómulo Gallegos Prize, and an honorary doctorate from Columbia University. In his native Colombia he became both a national hero and a household word. He was awarded the Nobel Prize for Literature in 1982.

Given the overwhelming popularity of *One Hundred Years of Solitude,* both the novice and the scholar of Latin-American literature may question its true aesthetic quality and lasting value. Several factors, however, support the proposition that García Márquez is a major writer of the twentieth century, rather than an ephemeral popularizer. Although his phenomenal rise in the international literary scene is remarkable, he also belongs to an established literary tradition.

One indication of García Márquez's true role within the movement of worldwide contemporary fiction is the volume of critical study that already has been dedicated to *One Hundred Years of Solitude* as well as to his other fictional writings. Studies dealing particularly with the Colombian novel, the Latin American novel, and those pertaining generally to world fiction give García Márquez a central position. Two book-length studies on the contemporary Colombian novel are necessarily organized with constant reference to the phenomenon of García Márquez in Colombia.[2] My own study of the Colombian novel of the 1970s takes up this phenomenon as a central issue.[3] John S. Brushwood's book on the twentieth-century Spanish-American novel treats *One Hundred Years of Solitude* as a key work of recent times.[4] Many American and European writers and critics point specifically to the importance of García Márquez. William Gass, for one prominent example, maintains that in the early 1970s many writers found in *One Hundred Years of Solitude* a sense of liberation that functioned as a kind of inspiration.[5]

The Rise of the New Novel and the Right of Invention in Spanish America

While it is often difficult for scholars to agree on a definition of literary movements or the exact dates of their beginning or ending, critics generally agree that there was a significant change in the quality and direction of the Spanish-American novel during the mid-1940s. The publication of four important novels indicated this new direction: *El Señor Presidente* (1946) by the Nobel Prize winning Guatemalan Miguel Angel Asturias, *Al filo del agua* (*At the Edge of the Storm,* 1947) by the Mexican Agustín Yáñez, *Adán Buenosayres* (1948) by the Argentine Leopoldo Marechal, and *El reino de este mundo* (*The Kingdom of this World*) by the Cuban Alejo Carpentier. At the beginning of this decade Adolfo Bioy Casares had published *La invención de Morel* (*The Invention of Morel*) with a prologue by Jorge Luis Borges. Excepting a few relatively disregarded and often unknown avant-garde novels published in the 1920s and 1930s, the Spanish-American novel before the upsurge noted above was limited to the mimetic portrayal of regional or national life and customs.

In terms of narrative technique, this fiction functioned within the boundaries of the realist tradition of the nineteenth century. The change that occurred in the late 1940s was basically the arrival on the scene of the modern novel, to a considerable extent using the innovations in fiction pioneered by Proust, Joyce, Dos Passos, Woolf, and Faulkner. Lino Novás Calvo, novelist and cultivator of the avant-garde in Cuba, published a translation of Faulkner's *Sanctuary* in 1934. Faulkner, as well as other writers commonly associated with modernism, was well-known among Latin-American intellectuals and writers by the 1930s.[6]

The recent history of Spanish-American fiction shows a regular continuity after the appearance of these four cornerstone novels in the late 1940s. Some of the most recognized novels to appear since then include Carpentier's *Los pasos perdidos* (*The Lost Steps,* 1953), Juan Rulfo's *Pedro Páramo* (1955), Carlos Fuentes's *La región más transparente* (*Where the Air is Clear,* 1958), Julio Cortazár's *Rayuela* (*Hopscotch,* 1963), Mario Vargas Llosa's *La casa verde* (*The Green House,* 1965), Guillermo Cabrera Infante's *Tres tristes tigres* (*Three Trapped Tigers,* 1967), and Manuel Puig's *La traición de Rita Hayworth* (*Betrayed by Rita Hayworth,* 1968), among many other superb novels written during this period and after. One salient characteristic of this new type of fiction in Spanish America was the insistence on the right of invention.[7] No longer content with reflecting reality, the Latin-American writer began to invent it.

Far from an isolated instance of brilliance, one may place García Márquez's work squarely within this tradition of Latin-American fiction, the insistence on this right of invention being his trademark. Given the relative lack of communication among Latin-American writers during the 1940s and 1950s, it is unlikely that García Márquez or any other Spanish-American writers were aware of what was happening to his fiction, generally considered.[8] Nevertheless, it is notable and not totally coincidental that García Márquez began publishing his first short stories in the late 1940s. The publication in 1955 of his first novel, *Leafstorm,* coincided with Rulfo's Spanish-American classic *Pedro Páramo.* Each is patently inventive and nonmimetic; Spanish-American fiction was a sophisticated and successful genre well before the publicized "boom" of the Spanish-American novel in which the excellence of this writing in general and García Márquez in particular was internationally recognized.

García Márquez and the Colombian Tradition

Colombia prides itself on being a stronghold of Spanish tradition. Colombians consider Bogotá the "Athens of South America." In the past the nation's relatively conservative attitude toward the arts and lack of a publishing house of international stature have limited the viability and visibility of the Colombian novel *extra muros,* so to speak. Argentina and Mexico, for example, have more recognized and probably more fully developed novelistic traditions. There are, of course, some notable exceptions to such a generalization, the major ones being Jorge Isaac's romantic novel *María* (1867), generally considered one of the finest novels of its type in nineteenth-century Spanish America, José Eustacio Rivera's *La vorágine* (*The Vortex,* 1924), and the development of fiction in the Caribbean coastal region of Colombia during the 1950s and 1960s. This latter category has been virtually ignored until recently; present-day awareness of it is due primarily to the place of García Márquez himself in the movement, seen in retrospect.

The persons involved in this Caribbean coastal movement are sometimes referred to as the "Group of Barranquilla." In opposition to the conservative attitudes implied in the imitation of Spanish tradition in Colombia and the identification of Bogotá as the "Athens of South America," the major city of the coastal region, Barranquilla, has been a more supportive environment for innovative and imaginative literature. One indication of the presence of the avant-garde in the region was the publication of a magazine entitled *Voces* in Barranquilla from 1917 to 1920. It included writings of Europeans such as Gide and Apollinaire, and such Latin-American avant-garde writers as José Juan Tablada and Vicente Huidobro. The principal thrust of Spanish-American fiction of the twenties featured the portrayal of the peculiarities of regional and national customs. Rivera's *La vorágine* is a traditional novel of this type. José Felix Fuenmayor of the coast, however, was more interested in invention. His short stories, as well as his novels *Cosme* (1927) and *Una triste aventura de 14 sabios* (A sad adventure of 14 wise men, 1928), contains an innovative use of narrative point of view and a playful, cosmopolitan attitude toward fiction.[9]

García Márquez not only belongs to this tradition of innovation but also was an admirer of Fuenmayor. In 1950 he wrote a journalistic note in praise of Fuenmayor's fiction.[10] The significant novelistic production of this coastal literature was García Márquez's *Leafstorm*, Alvaro Cepeda Samudio's *La casa grande* (The big house, 1962), and Héctor Rojas Herazo's *Respirando el verano* (Breathing the summer, 1962).[11] Each is a Faulknerian-type novel, as is particularly apparent in the structure and use of narrative point of view. *Leafstorm* reflects García Márquez's readings of Faulkner during the late 1940s with his companions of the group. Even though some of the exact details of readings and personalities vary according to the particular witness or investigator, there is absolutely no question that García Márquez spent the late 1940s reading and learning from Faulkner and other modern writers. Ramón Vinyes, a Catalan who will later appear as a character in *One Hundred Years of Solitude,* functioned as a literary father figure for García Márquez and his friends who met regularly at the Japy Bar or La Cueva to discuss their latest readings and writing. Germán Vargas, a member of the group, has described the situation as follows:

For several years we were colleagues at the newspaper of Julian Devis, to which I returned when I met Alvaro Cepeda [Samudio]. Before settling on La Cueva we had several different meeting places: the Café Colombia, the Japy—written just like that—Los Almendros, a strange bar which was called El Tercer Hombre, the América-Billares. It already was what Próspero Morales Pradilla called, from [the newspaper] *El Tiempo,* the Group of Barranquilla. Everything centered on the great Catalonian writer Ramón Vinyes, the wise Catalan from *One Hundred Years of Solitude.*[12]

Vinyes was the motivating force behind the publication of the magazine *Voces.* García Márquez's participation in the group's discussions and the subsequent development of his literary career leads to a more detailed consideration of his biography.

A Biographical Overview

García Márquez claims to have learned everything that was important in his life by the time he was eight years old. Setting aside his literary apprenticeship, that claim could be true. He was born in Aracataca, a small town in the Caribbean coastal region, on 6 March 1928. The first eight years were special because he spent them with his grandparents. His father, a telegrapher, left Aracataca with the rest of the family, leaving Gabriel to hear the myths and legends of Aracataca as told by his grandfather.

Both Aracataca and the family's home lent themselves easily to storytelling. The grandparents, according to García Márquez, "had an enormous house, full of ghosts. They were very susperstitious and impressionable people. In every corner there were skeletons and memories, and after six in the evening you didn't dare leave your room. It was a world of fantastic terrors. There were coded conversations."[13] The town had somehow survived the devastating War of a Thousand Days (1899–1902), one of the bloodiest of the numerous civil wars between Liberals and Conservatives during the nineteenth century. Gabriel's grandfather recounted the exploits of one of Colombia's national heroes from this war, General Rafael Uribe Uribe. Colombians still tell stories about the supposed thirty-six battles he fought, losing them all. General Uribe Uribe would serve years later as the model for Colonel Aureliano Buendía in *One Hundred Years of Solitude*. When Gabriel was born, Aracataca had just completed a period of economic boom with the "banana fever" of the two decades prior to his birth. The prosperity and "progress" brought by the Americans were just as ephemeral as they were sudden in their arrival and disappearance. The sense of emptiness left by this "leafstorm" of vanished modernity was communicated orally to the young Gabriel, later to be utilized as a central image in his first novel, *Leafstorm*. He also heard different versions of the massacre of striking banana workers in 1928 in Ciénaga, a small coastal town. The government sent soldiers to break the strike, resulting in the death of many workers—the versions of the story range from hundreds to thousands, the latter probably being closer to reality. This historical act appears in *One Hundred Years of Solitude* with all the ambiguity of the actual event.

Stories such as these were the material on which the anecdotes—historical, legendary, mythical—were based. Although the grandfather was the principal storyteller, apparently Gabriel's grandmother was an exceptional woman, particularly in the spontaneity and naturalness with which she could spin yarns. This knack for reacting to the most incredible things with absolute naturalness is an aspect of *One Hundred Years of Solitude* that García Márquez considers a key to the tone of his masterpiece. It was a key that took nearly twenty years of writing to discover.

García Márquez maintains that neither his own writing nor that of other highly imaginative Latin-American writers is a product of pure fantasy. Latin-American reality, rather, has a magic that writers capture in their fictional description.[14] The coastal region where García Márquez spent his youth is a setting par excellence for this magical reality. A synthesis of African and Hispanic cultures, with aspects of all centuries from the Middle Ages to the present, this region is viewed even by Colombians as a distinct and exotic part of the nation. It is still common for males in this region, for example, to support several women and father thirty or forty children. Readers already acquainted with *One Hundred Years of Solitude* or Colombians from the coast do not find such facts at all surprising. This fact makes the sexual prowess of Colonel Aureliano Buendía sound less fantastic. The medieval sense of honor that is a central motif in *Chronicle of a Death Foretold* is commonplace in much of Latin America: García Márquez based the novel on an actual murder-for-honor story that was published in a Colombian newspaper.[15] In this area, not only can fiction be as real as fantastic life, but also fantastic life can be as real as fiction. After the publication of *One Hundred Years of Solitude*, tellingly enough, García Márquez received a letter from a person born with a pig's tail, one of the novel's seemingly "fantastic" events.

García Márquez had to exchange life in this vital and fabulous coast for the frigid climate and people of Bogotá, located high in the Andes. His parents sent him to complete his secondary education in Zipaquirá, a town near Bogotá, and there he received his high school degree from a private Jesuit school in 1946. After a brief visit to the coast, he returned to Bogotá in 1947 to pursue studies of law at the National University. Two events, however, were to make 1947 more important for his future literary career than for jurisprudence. First, he met Plinio Apuleyo Mendoza, who would be a supporter in García Márquez's nascent years as a writer and prove a valued colleague and collaborator later. More specifically, he and García Márquez were later reunited in Paris in the late 1950s when the latter was struggling to become established as a writer. After some years, he published a book of conversations with this friend of literary adolescence, *The Fragrance of Guava.*

García Márquez also penned his first story in 1947, "La tercera resignación" ("The Third Resignation"). This story and others that would soon follow appeared in Bogotá's newspaper *El Espectador.* Within the next five years he published a total of fifteen stories in *El Espectador, Crónica,* and *El Heraldo.* "La tercera resignación," like the other stories, was more important as a symbolic beginning than for its artistic merit. (For analysis of the story, see chapter 2.) Critics have gone to considerable lengths to demonstrate the influence of certain writers in these early stories, particularly that of Kafka and Faulkner. This labor can be explained by the traditional curiosity in the original sources of a major writer. In addition, the critic feels almost compelled to mention these writers because García Márquez blatantly transferred his reading to what he was writing.

The young García Márquez's reading during this period was determined by a series of events that later placed him in contact with an enlightened group of intellectuals and writers. In April 1949 the course of Colombia's history and García Márquez's career were altered considerably by the assassination of the Liberal party's populist candidate for the presidency, Jorge Eliécer Gaitán. Immediate chaos in Bogotá was followed by years of armed conflict and civil war between Liberals and Conservatives, mostly in rural areas. Colombians call this period from approximately 1948 to 1958 *la violencia,* although these exact dates are somewhat arbitrary. One immediate effect of the instability in Bogotá was García Márquez's change in residence to Cartagena, back on the coast. *La violencia* is never a central focus in García Márquez's fiction, but is present in much of it, especially *In Evil Hour.* By June 1948 García Márquez enrolled in the National University of Cartagena to continue law studies, where he also wrote for Cartagena's newspaper, *El Universal.*

These were crucial years for García Márquez's literary apprenticeship and initial development as a writer. The very first stories represented his efforts to create the experience of terror and exercise the right of invention he had observed in the stories of Kafka. On the coast he began to read even more widely. One can document García Márquez's first written acknowledgment of Faulkner approximately one year after his arrival (28 July 1949); the young Colombian writer names Faulkner in a newspaper article.[16] The same year "A Rose for Emily" appeared in translation, quite possibly Faulkner's first work read by García Márquez.[17] García Márquez put Faulkner's influence in dramatic terms: "When I first read Faulkner, I thought: I must become a writer."[18]

During this period García Márquez's friends were his tutors and teachers. In 1950 he moved to nearby Barranquilla where he wrote for *El Heraldo.* Most important, he met with that group of friends already identified as the Group of Barranquilla. They discussed their latest readings of writers such as Faulkner, Virginia Woolf, Dos

Passos, Hemingway, and others. This enlightened group of aspiring writers included Alfonso Fuenmayor (José Felix Fuenmayor's son), Alvaro Cepeda Samudio, and Germán Vargas. The already mentioned Ramón Vinyes introduced the young writers to the most recent innovations of the avant-garde in world fiction. His important role in the development of what has been a general upsurge of writing on the coast has subsequently caused Vinyes to assume the stature of a legendary figure in Colombia.[9]

By the early 1950s García Márquez was beginning to take himself seriously as a writer. He had rejected a possible career in law after three years of study. In addition to the comprehensive readings and regular publication of stories, a first novel was taking form. Argentina's prestigious Losada publishing house rejected this manuscript, a novel entitled "La casa." For García Márquez, the usefulness and intellectual vitality of the coast had been exhausted by the early 1950s: the excitement of new readings in fiction and initial publications was over; the seeming culmination of the early stage of his career, the novel, had been rejected. García Márquez's friend Alvaro Mutis invited him to return to Bogotá to write for *El Espectador*. It is not surprising that he accepted, arriving in the capital in February 1954.

Within a year after his return to Bogotá, everything started to acquire a more positive tone. Several factors provided an initial opportunity for international visibility, although such exposure was, at this point, extremely limited. Most important, the first novel was published, under the title *Leafstorm*. Several contradictory reports are available about this first book's initial impact in Colombia. There are, in fact, numerous versions about many aspects of García Márquez's life and work, some of which have been propagated by García Márquez himself. Luis Harss, who has interviewed him extensively, provides an excellent understanding of this problem: "His facts are provisional, valid not as statements but as assumptions, what he feels today he may discard tomorrow."[20] An acquaintance with the Colombian literary scene supports Mario Vargas Llosa's explanation of *Leafstorm*'s impact in Colombia: it was sparsely circulated and elicited very little critical reaction.[21] Although the novel was his most noteworthy literary accomplishment to that date, other factors provided more visibility and impetus to his still-fledgling and unsure literary career. The Association of Artists and Writers of Bogotá awarded him a prize for his story "Un día después del sábado" ("One Day After Saturday"). The combination of this prize with the publication of the first novel make 1955 the year perhaps best suited to describe García Márquez as a "writer." Before this he was a student and professional journalist first, amateur writer second.

Just as significant as the publications was the opportunity to distance himself from Colombia's immediate situation, the intensity of *la violencia* that at least indirectly affected all Colombians. In July of 1955, *El Espectador* sent García Márquez to Geneva. The military government in Colombia closed the newspaper soon afterward, leaving him stranded in Europe. After a brief stay in Rome, García Márquez moved to Paris where he struggled with his writing and with finding a base level of subsistence. There are stories of his collecting bottles in the streets of Paris in order to pay for food. For the next three years he lived in Paris unemployed and worked on the manuscripts for *In Evil Hour* and *No One Writes to the Colonel*. If distance from Colombia and the new experiences were indeed significant in his development as a writer, García Márquez took advantage of a series of totally new experiences during these years. In addition to the cosmopolitan atmosphere of Paris—in stark contrast to the traditional and hermetic Colombia, especially Bogotá—García Márquez traveled through the Eastern European countries, including the Soviet Union, whose Slavic cultures and socialist governments could not have been a more different world from tropical, Hispanic, and capitalist Colombia.

The years in Europe were García Márquez's first extended period devoted exclusively to the proposition of writing fiction. The work completed during this time was one more important step toward the total fictionalization of Macondo that would appear in *One Hundred Years of Solitude*. This step in the creation of Macondo was the writing of the stories of *Big Mama's Funeral*. This last period prior to the creation of his masterpiece comprises roughly 1958 to 1962. García Márquez's travels and positions during this four-year period took him from Europe to Caracas, Colombia, the United States, and Mexico. In addition to the stories of *Big Mama's Funeral,* the period also saw the publication of *No One Writes to the Colonel* and *In Evil Hour*. The Cuban Revolution in 1959 was celebrated by most Latin-American intellectuals, including García Márquez, and resulted in his working as a journalist for Cuba's press agency, Prensa Latina, from 1959 to 1961.

García Márquez traveled by bus from New York to Mexico in 1961 with his wife of three years, Mercedes, and son. This bus trip through the South was his "homage to Faulkner." The observer of García Márquez's career in the early 1960s might have guessed that the voyage was García Márquez's final tribute to literature, and with good reason. His writing had exerted virtually no impact outside Colombia and relatively little in his homeland, beyond the group of intellectuals and friends who read his novels and noticed the national prizes he had won. Even García Márquez himself was not planning to write any more fiction after 1962.[22] The years from 1962 to 1965 were not only devoid of literary publications, but also barren of serious fictional creation. Like Faulkner at a similar stage of his career, however, García Márquez did write some film scripts.

The magical world of Macondo somehow began to coalesce, almost in his subconscious, in 1965. García Márquez tells of spontaneously discovering the key to the fictional world for which, in effect, he had been striving since writing *Leafstorm*.[23] He went into seclusion in his home in Mexico with the conviction that his masterpiece finally was to be produced and with the confidence to pursue the year-long project on a full-time basis. Mercedes protected him against interruption during this period of isolation. One key to the successful synthesis of the different elements of Macondo into one magnificent whole was at least in part a result of a fortunate confluence of personal biography and literary practice: that special attitude toward reality learned from his grandmother, an attitude of naturalness and indifference toward absolutely anything, a unique feature of *One Hundred Years of Solitude*. By 1966 rumors about García Márquez's literary bombshell were already in circulation. Carlos Fuentes and Julio Cortázar had read fragments and endorsed the novel enthusiastically in print even before its publication. When it appeared in Buenos Aires in May 1967, the literary explosion described by Vargas Llosa at the beginning of this chapter ensued.

García Márquez's life changed radically as he was thrust into the international limelight. Invitations to conferences and other accolades made it difficult to maintain the level of privacy that García Márquez, fundamentally a private person, preferred. In August he met Mario Vargas Llosa in Caracas for the first time. After the literary symposium in Caracas the two went to Bogatá and Lima. In Lima they participated in a round-table discussion on the novel,

later published as *La novela en América Latina: un diálogo* (1968).
The "boom" was at full apogee.

Since attaining his now international recognition, García Márquez
has lived in or between Colombia, Spain, and Mexico, mostly in
the latter. Success has involved the translation not only of *One
Hundred Years of Solitude,* but also much of his previous work—
fiction which, ironically, readers and critics almost entirely ignored
until 1967. Faced with the inevitable problem of how to follow up
on the masterpiece with a work of similar quality, García Márquez
has written little since 1967; he delayed eight years before the
publication of another novel.

One Hundred Years of Solitude had culminated the cycle of Macondo;
García Márquez's career after 1967 has been dedicated to writing
beyond Macondo. All the stories except one of the original Spanish
volume *The Incredible and Sad Tale of Innocent Erendira and Her Heartless Grandmother* (1972) were written after 1967 and do not use
Macondo as a setting. The long-awaited novel finally appeared in
1975, *The Autumn of the Patriarch.* Just as *One Hundred Years of
Solitude* represented a culmination of the cycle of Macondo, *The
Autumn of the Patriarch* was the result of a project that had appealed
to García Márquez for many years: a novel about a dictator. Such
a novel was an idea he had been cultivating since experiencing the
end of the dictatorship of Pérez Jiménez in Venezuela in 1958.
Other sources made the novel most timely: there was already a certain
Hispanic tradition of fiction of this type, and other Latin American
writers enjoying the "boom" in Latin-American literature, such as
Alejo Carpentier and Augusto Roa Bastos, were preparing novelistic
denunciations of dictatorships.

Given his newly acquired fame, García Márquez's political activ-
ism was more visible in the 1970s. As his work with Prensa Latina
after the Cuban Revolution testifies, he had been a supporter of
leftist causes since the initial euphoria among Latin-American intellectuals at the outset of the Revolution. Even the singularly
discouraging political climate of the 1970s, when rightist military
regimes dominated Latin American politics, García Márquez remained active. He began to publish the political magazine *Alternativa* in Colombia in 1974, an organ intended to propagate radical
social change in Colombia and Latin America. García Márquez pub-
licly denounced the dictatorship of Augusto Pinochet in Chile by
claiming in 1975, soon after the appearance of *The Autumn of the*

Patriarch, that he would not publish another novel until after Pinochet was overthrown.

As suggested already, García Márquez's public statements are often either misleading or contradictory. Such is the case of the pronouncement concerning Pinochet and further novels, for in 1981 Pinochet was still firmly in power and *Chronicle of a Death Foretold* indeed was published. In reality, García Márquez felt by 1975 that he had probably already written all the novels he had ever desired to create and preferred to devote himself to journalism.[24] This sense toward his work was basically correct; his latest novel is short and relatively insignificant within the context of his total fiction. His life, his public declarations, and his political postures are in many ways fascinating in themselves, exceptional, and useful for an understanding and fuller appreciation of his work. In the final analysis, however, each of these matters is noteworthy only because of the fiction that García Márquez published. The following chapters will provide a chronological overview and analysis of this total work.

Chapter Two
The Early Fiction (1948–55)

The First Stories (1947–52)

García Márquez's fiction published from 1947 to 1955 marked a period from his first inventions to the establishment of his professional identity as a writer by the mid-1950s. The first stories, as has been suggested, were more important as a symbolic beginning than for their purely artistic merit. But with their publication García Márquez began to take himself seriously as a writer, and soon thereafter began his first novel.

The stories from the 1947–52 period are mostly unknown beyond the Hispanic world and relatively ignored by critics, even among Hispanists.[1] The fact that some of them were García Márquez's only untranslated fiction when he won the Nobel Prize in 1982 is more a reflection of their occasional amateurish qualities than the ignorance of the critics or translators. Viewed retrospectively as the first creations of a future Nobel-Prize winning author with universal appeal, they are revealing pieces of fiction.

García Márquez's readings of Kafka during the 1940s allowed the discovery that literature can not only reflect reality, but also permit the invention of reality; fiction can not only present moral problems in social contexts, but also place into question the matter of reality itself. In his first story, "La tercera resignación" ("The Third Resignation"), he attempts to create a literature like Kafka's that defies the rational limits of what is normally accepted as everyday reality. The story deals with a man who is apparently dead, but who seems to function on some gray area between the normal categories of life and death. The story's initial frame of reference is totally interior, psychological. At the outset the exact circumstances of the protagonist are ambiguous and even confusing: he suffers from something which the reader is not able to clarify in the first three paragraphs. In the third paragraph the ambiguity becomes a frontal attack on our rational sense of the reality of the story: "Había sentido ese ruido 'las otras veces', con la misma insistencia. Lo había sentido, por ejemplo, el día en que murió por primera vez"[2] ("He had heard the noise with the same insistence 'at other times.' He had heard it, for instance, on the day he had died for the first time").[3] The remainder of the story elaborates on this peculiar state which the narrator identifies as a "living death."

The peculiarity and eeriness of this "living death" recall the horrors of Kafka. There are other suggestions that the author of this story was struggling to create a Kafkaesque world. Immediately before the revelation concerning the "living death," the narrator states the following: "Pero le era imposible apretarse las sienes. Sus brazos se habían reducido y eran ahora los brazos de un enano; unos brazos pequeños, regordetes, adiposos" ("But it was impossible for him to squeeze his temples. His arms had been shortened on him and were now the limbs of a dwarf; small, chubby, adipose arms," 95). Soon the narrative seems to move to a more "real" level of reality of our everyday, empirical world: the narrator returns to the past scene of the protagonist's death. The doctor appears to articulate an explanation of the situation with all the professional's traditional serenity and rationality: "Señora, su niño tiene una enfermedad grave: está muerto" ("Madam, your child has a grave illness: he is dead," 96). There is a certain oddity in his equating death with even a "serious" sickness, however. His discourse becomes totally irrational as he continues, returning the reader to the Kafkaesque world of the unreal: "Sin embargo, haremos todo lo posible por conservarle la vida más allá de su muerte" ("Nevertheless, we shall do everything possible to keep him alive beyond death," 96–97).

In this story García Márquez is overtly preoccupied with the creation of "another reality," along the lines of what he had recently experienced in his readings of contemporary writers. One brief passage in the story not only demonstrates this interest or fictional goal explicitly, but also reveals him as the nineteen-year-old amateur writer that he was. He falls into the use of a more directly expositional rather than descriptive discourse:

Allí había empezado una especie de vacío en su vida. Desde entonces no podía distinguir, recordar cuáles acontecimientos eran parte de su delirio y cuáles de su vida real. Por tanto, ahora dudaba. Tal vez el médico habló de esa extraña "muerta viva." Es ilógica, paradojal, sencillamente contradictoria. Y eso lo hacía sospechar que, efectivamente, estaba muerto de verdad.

A kind of emptiness in his life had begun there. From then on he had been unable to distinguish, to remember what events were part of his delirium and what were part of his real life. That was why he doubted now. Perhaps the doctor had never mentioned that strange "living death." It was illogical, paradoxical, simply contradictory. And it made him suspect now that he really was dead. (97)

In these lines García Márquez directly communicates his desire to create a Kafkaesque fiction. Unlike Kafka, however, he does not create the experience for the reader of the illogical, the paradoxical, and the contradictory. Instead, he simply enumerates such sensations—actually utilizing the words "illogical," "paradoxical," and "contradictory."

Despite this defect, it is interesting in several ways, especially as a first story. The brief deviation indicates clearly what García Márquez's literary goals were from his first story: in addition to being aware of his own national reality (which will surface in all his later work), he was interested in creating experiences that would not be limited to political boundaries. As a participant in the Colombian coastal tradition, and as a reader of modern fiction, he was fascinated by the universally human experience. In addition, it is a surprisingly well crafted piece of fiction for a first story. It is extremely coherent, for example, with respect to the handling of narrative point of view.[4] García Márquez resists—except for the passage noted above—the temptation to interrupt the narrative to comment editorially, or perhaps clarify.

The remainder of the stories written during this 1948–52 period share several of the characteristics, accomplishments, and defects noted above. They show a writer experimenting with the potentiality of different uses of narrative point of view. These variations include a neutral omniscient narrator who reveals the characters psychologically (such as in "La tercera resignación"), first-person narrations, and combinations of the two. In "La otra costilla de la muerte" ("The Other Side of Death") for example, the story is basically narrated in third person, but the author is consciously working with the use of both his point of view and first-person interiorization, a type of interior monologue. García Márquez invents other oddities with respect to just point of view: a story with three blind narrators; one with a dead narrator; another with a multiple "we" narrator representing three characters. Virtually all these early stories take place in a rarefied, fantastic world, such as "La tercera resignación," in contrast to our everyday empirical world of cause and effect. Mario Vargas Llosa has noted another common thread: a metaphysical-masturbatory scheme is repeated throughout the stories.[5] A solitary character tortures himself with thoughts of ontological disintegration, duplication, or extinction. Such a generalization holds true in all but two stories.

"La otra costilla de la muerte" represents another overt attempt to create "another reality," but with a different approach. It deals with a man who seems to suffer from insomnia after the death of his twin brother. The beginning places the reader in the unstable oneiric world of the first story: the character travels through a countryside "de naturalezas mentales, sembrado de árboles artificiales, falsos, frutecidos de navajas, tijeras . . . ." ("like a still life, sown with false, artificial trees bearing fruit of razors, scissors, . . ." 107). After a series of such shocking images, the man realizes that he is terrorized by the image of his brother suffering the agony of death. For the first time he thinks about the heredity which links him with his brother and, more surprisingly, the possibility that part of his own self could find itself dead with his brother. He concludes that he will eventually rot with his brother. At first such a thought horrifies him, but he gradually becomes attracted to the simplicity of death, until at the end of the story he resigns himself to death.

The intercalation of interior monologues within the third-person narration creates a closeness to the oneiric and terrifying effects of the situation for the reader. The use of the two narrators also maintains the sensation of confusion established in the opening section of the story. In addition, this alteration of narrative point of view emphasizes the conflict between exterior reality, described in third person, and the interior, psychological reality of first person.

The young writer reveals his intentions, once again, with a language that explicitly embodies irrational concepts of space and time, rather than creating such experiences for the reader. García Márquez is not yet capable of making time stop for the reader, but demonstrates his interest in doing so when he observes: "El tiempo parecía haberse detenido al borde de la madrugada" (23) ("Time seemed to have stopped on the edge of dawn," 111). The last line of the story is both a conclusive portrayal of the protagonist existing in a very special state and a direct articulation of his literary goals:

"Resignado, oyó la gota, pesada, exacta, que golpeaba en el otro mundo, en el mundo equivocado y absurdo de los animales racionales . . ." (27) ("Resigned, he listened to the drop, thick, heavy, exact, as it dripped in the other world, in the mistaken and absurd world of rational creatures," 116).

The portrayal of an absurd and irrational world is also both the goal and effect of one of the longest of these early stories, "Eva está dentro de su gato" ("Eva Is Inside Her Cat"). Indeed, it is essentially the same story communicated in the two previous ones, with a change in character. This character, Eva, lives in a world in which all "dimensions" have been eliminated. It is a type of limbo that seems to be in touch with both the "real" world and another world in death. She remembers that spirits can be reincarnated in living bodies, and decides to be reborn in her cat. At this point the story takes yet another step toward the fantastic within the realm of the fantastic: she discovers that neither the cat nor her house exists any longer: three thousand years have passed since she lived in the world of life. As in all fantastic literature, of course, this series of events, as well as her state of existence, is inexplicable. The narrator himself emphasizes this point for the reader, who happens to be as innocent as the author of the story: "No podría dar ninguna explicación, aclarar nada, consolar a nadie" (36) ("She wouldn't be able to give any explanation, clear anything up, console anybody," 126).

"Diálogo del espejo" ("Dialogue with the Mirror") and "Tubal-Caín forja una estrella" (Tubal-caín forges a star) are exercises in modernist literature par excellence. They function on the basis of different schemes. The former deals with a businessman who arises and prepares himself for a day at the office. His sense of pettiness and monotony is typical of the literature of the ennui of modern bourgeois life. It uses as its point of departure a real-world setting and then exploits another level of reality through the doubling effect the protagonist experiences observing himself in the bathroom mirror. García Márquez's discovery of the double as a literary mechanism is a step in his apprenticeship that will be useful later, and much more adroitly exploited too. Whereas the basic scheme for "Diálogo del espejo" is the double, in "Tubal-Caín forja una estrella" it is free association. The apparent incoherence and unconnected ideas make it a classic piece of youthful experimentation with language, albeit basically unsuccessful; it is one of the weakest stories of those written in this period.

Two stories told by first-person narrators, "Ojos de perro azul" ("Eyes of a Blue Dog") and "Alguien desordena estas rosas" ("Someone Has Been Disarranging These Roses") evoke vastly different effects. The former, written in 1950, portrays a situation reflecting French existentialist literature: its point of departure is two persons isolated in a room. The male narrator-protagonist observes a nude woman. The stark surroundings are matched by their frigid dialogue. The woman's comment that she sometimes seems "metallic" to herself, then, seems appropriate. The situation moves to the past and a more dreamlike world. The eyes of a blue dog of the title refer to the fact that during a dream the man had seen a woman whose eyes surprised him. The interesting point with respect to the reality games that were a significant element in this early fiction is that the couple continue seeing each other in their dreams. The reader can legitimately question if García Márquez has perhaps surpassed playful ambiguity to attain total confusion: does the woman, for example, really seek the man in the "real" world of the protagonist-narrator? Vargas Llosa appropriately considers this the weakest in style and structure of the stories written during this period.[6]

A first-person narrator in "Alguien desordena estas rosas," in contrast, serves as the basis for one of the most successful of the early stories. The special nature of the situation, the fact that the narrator is dead, is established in the story's first line: "Como es domingo y ha dejado de llover, pienso llevar un ramo de rosas a mi tumba" 85) ("Since it's Sunday and it's stopped raining, I think I'll take a bouquet of roses to my grave" 171). Apart from this fact, which the reader accepts from the beginning, the story functions in a real world, in contrast to the fantastic of the other stories. This dead voice that announces in the first line that it will carry a bouquet of flowers to the tomb is in fact the voice of a little boy who had died forty years before, falling down a staircase. For the past twenty years he has lived with the woman who had been his faithful childhood friend. The house has a small chapel and each Sunday a breeze places the flowers on this altar in disarray. In reality the cause of the disheveled flowers is the spirit of this boy, who each Sunday tries in vain to take a bouquet of roses from the house to his own tomb. This story seems to resemble the fables of ambulatory ghosts of the sort that García Márquez heard from his grandparents in that house supposedly full of ghosts. Indeed, this story represents a notable transition from the horror-fantasy of those first stories to

what will later be the literature of Macondo. Published in 1952, it
is more Faulknerian in tone and technique than the initial stories
from the late 1940s. The use of a first-person narrator as a technical
device to create suspense is quite likely a lesson learned from the
reading of Faulkner. The story is not totally clarified, for example,
until the last line of the story: "Porque ese día sabía que no era el
viento invisible lo que todos los domingos llegaba a su altar y le
desordenaba las rosas," 89) ("Because on that day she'll learn that
it wasn't the invisible wind that came to her altar every Sunday and
disarranged the roses," 176).

"Alguien desordena estas rosas" belongs to the period when García
Márquez's fiction of Macondo was beginning to take form. This
story, which uses the special ambience of a home as its base, corresponds strikingly to the situation in *Leafstorm,* the novel that
officially initiates the cycle of Macondo. Both the rough draft for
Leafstorm and this story were written in the early 1950s.

Two other stories function even more on the plane of a "real
reality," "Nabo el negro que hizo esperar a los ángeles" ("Nabo,
the Black Who Made the Angels Wait"), and "Amargura para tres
sonámbulos" ("Bitterness for Three Sleepwalkers"). "Nabo" seems
like something written by a reader of Faulkner both because of its
narrative technique and its setting in a Deep South—type ambience,
replete with the plantation, black slaves, and a genteel aristocracy.
Nabo, the protagonist, is a black whose main duties on the plantation are brushing the horses and playing music to entertain a
mentally retarded girl. Actually, this situation is not clear to the
reader until the story is well advanced.

The story begins with a much more enigmatic situation: someone
who is nearly unconscious is lying on the ground, and the reader
is privy to some of the sensations he feels in this state. Rather than
moving to some other fantastic state as in many of the other stories,
however, the story develops in the direction of a concrete reality:
this person is identified as Nabo, a character who lies on the ground
semiunconscious after having suffered a kick in the head from a
horse. He is mentally deficient for the rest of his life. The plantation
owners tie him up in a room and leave him for fifteen years, passing
a plate of food under the door three times a day. Nabo puts an end
to this period of imprisonment by breaking out one day, savagely
destroying virtually everything in sight. He sees the woman who
had been his audience as a little girl and she utters the only word

she knows: "Nabo." The end of the story relates this series of events in a more interior fashion, recapitulating Nabo's thoughts in such a way that it could well be total fantasy.

"Nabo" has some truly incredible details, such as the extended period of imprisonment and even worse, the three meals a day shoved under the door—followed by the regular returning of empty plates. Nevertheless, the realm of the story is the concrete empirical world rather than the fantastic. In this sense "Nabo" is an early example of García Márquez's imaginative incorporation of surprising and incredible events into a very everyday world—and without the slightest hesitation.

"Amargura para tres sonámbulos" is also located in an everyday reality and is almost as incredible. It is about a girl who fell from the second story of a house, becoming permanently deformed and crippled. The first-person plural narrators tell of her in a type of elegy. The situation is presented but not explained in the opening paragraph: she is simply "sentada en un rincón" ("abandoned in a corner of the house," 140). Like narrators in many of García Márquez's later stories, the three brothers who relate this story are not surprised by anything. Nevertheless, she makes a series of rather astonishing affirmations, such as "No volveré a sonreir" ("I won't smile again") and "No volveré a ver" ("I won't see again"). Parallel to the location of this story in a concrete, real world, the language is less vague and opaque than in many of the fantastic stories—this direct style is much more refined.

An initial reading or superficial description of these stories virtually precludes relating them to the inventor of Macondo. Vargas Llosa claims that a reading of these stories makes it difficult to believe they were first steps in his literary career.[7] Their overt experimentation with universal experience and sense of play with reality itself, however, point to a writer conscientiously creating something for consumption beyond narrow national boundaries. His incursions into "another reality" are the best examples of this fact.

The use of a complex set of narrative situations implies more than just an interest in technical experimentation. The structure of non-linear development in conjunction with the multiple points of view creates an experiential-type literature: the reader experiences reality turned upside-down in "La tercera resignación," for example, rather than just observing it. In addition, as one theorist of fiction has aptly pointed out, ideology is not just a matter of thematic content

"poured into" a text, but is the very fabric of textual organization.[8]
On the basis of this observation is it possible to recognize in García
Márquez the potential which narrative point of view holds for ex-
pressing its ideological base.

A first step in the recognition of this ideological potential lies in
the observation that structure and point of view in these stories
work toward the breakdown of the bases on which modern rational
society functions. García Márquez is working toward a modern
literature that, in effect, questions all assumptions. It marks an
initial step toward a total lack of faith in purely rational tools.
García Márquez portrays a confusing and decadent society in these
early stories. This fiction is a first step toward a literature that
should be seen not as an organically homogeneous entity, but rather
as a symbolic act that attempts to harmonize elements that are
ideologically heterogeneous.[9] There are traces of that real Colombian
context that locate the story in Latin America. One type of heterogeneity is articulated in the concomitant space of the fantastic,
that striving for "another reality" to achieve goals vastly different
from the mere portrayal of social realities. The reader perceives the
contrast between the static, hierarchical society of Latin America
and the dynamic movement of modern societies from which the
literature of modernism, such as Kafka's, was being initially gen-
erated. The Colombia of the 1940s and 1950s contained both traditional and modern elements, in perfect juxtaposition. Even the
pictures which the tourist sees of skyscrapers next to sixteenth-
century churches in Bogotá, for example, or donkeys in the streets
in front of new automobiles, are telling examples of the heterogeneity and anachronism of Latin American society.

In Bakhtin's terms, the heterogeneity of these stories is a response
to the basic condition governing the operation of meaning in any
utterance—heteroglossia.[10] Heteroglossia is in opposition to a concept of a static unitary language. Rather, it is language as a continuous flux of incorporated languages. Dialogism—the mode of a
world dominated by heteroglossia—is abundant in these early stories. On the one hand, this world of heteroglossia involves the
incorporation of several identifiable literary modes—more specifically, those of Kafka, Faulkner, and Sartre. A story such as "Tubal-
Caín" represents an effort to undermine any traditional concept of
unitary literary language.

This commentary may make these stories sound more sophisticated than they really are for the reader acquainted with them. In some cases, they are more a matter of pretension and future promises than of successful writing. The variety of technical features and thematic concerns does not result in a consistently accomplished fiction at this stage. The weak point here—common to many if not all beginning writers—can be explained to a large extent by noting that García Márquez had not yet learned how to characterize one of the most important of all literary personas—the reader. As Walter Ong has convincingly explained, a successful writer must be able to fictionalize a reader whose role the real reader finds attractive to play.[11] García Márquez demonstrates an admirable ability to manipulate narrative techniques; nevertheless, he is only beginning, in stories like "Nabo," to master the more delicate matter of characterizing the reader.

The Later Stories

The two stories published in 1955 demonstrate radical changes from the stories of the adolescent writer. Most important, within the context of García Márquez's total writing career, is the invention of Macondo. This marvelous town will provide a clearly defined Latin American geographical setting, rather than the abstract spaces of the first stories. Macondo will be further defined and invented for some ten years. These two stories naturally also reflect some of the themes and techniques of the earlier stories.

"Monologue of Isabel Watching It Rain in Macondo" is a first-person narration which tells the story of Macondo's being inundated by rain. Given the constant presence of rain in García Márquez's later fiction (it will be important in *No One Writes to the Colonel* and *One Hundred Years of Solitude*), it is perhaps appropriate that the first paragraph of the first story about Macondo deal with rain. The monologue covers five days, Sunday through Thursday, a period during which the situation in Macondo, due to the rains, becomes progressively worse. The narrator-protagonist's perception of the general situation and her own particular circumstance make the story more than just a tale about a town's confrontation with a physical disaster.

The story begins with the rain: "El invierno se precipitó un domingo a la salida de misa,"[12] ("Winter fell one Sunday when people were coming out of church"). [13] From the moment they leave church they run to cover from the cloudburst. Isabel finds the new water refreshing at first and her father interprets it as a sign that there will be ample water for the year. As the rain continues, the narrator contemplates the past, the hot days of August before the rains. She, like the remainder of the family, watches the rain in boredom as she also awaits the birth of a son. By Tuesday a cow appears, and the Indians are ordered to scare it off; they do not succeed. The continuous flow of the rain seems to affect and even pain the protagonist. The family grows numbed and insensitive from the rain, as its monotony wears on them. They reach a point by Thursday at which their only functional sense is that of touch. The end of the story contains a final surprise: both the narrator and the reader discover that she in fact is dead.

The details of the development of this story reveal a series of subtle changes that reflect the progressive deteriorization of the family. In fact, the entire story is a process of breaking down any sense of homogeneous unity. The first change—the weather—seems insignificant at first. The initial reactions of the people are mundane and natural enough: they look for their umbrellas and cover. The first indication of García Márquez's *modus operandi* appears in the last sentence of the first paragraph: "Y el cielo fue una sustancia gelatinosa y gris que aleteó a una cuarta de nuestras cabezas" ("And the sky was gray, jellyish substance that flapped its wings a hand away from our heads," 197). The equation of "cielo" ("sky") with "sustancia gelatinosa" ("jellyish substance") is interpreted in the first reading as a fairly standard metaphor. In reality, it is the first step in a process of literal transformation of the physical world, rather than a metaphorical transformation.

The physical environment soon has its initial effects on the mental state of the characters. At first this impact seems natural enough. The narrator explains: "Pero sin que lo advirtiéramos, la lluvia estaba penetrando demasiado hondo en nuestros sentidos," (98) ("But without our noticing it, the rain was penetrating too deeply into our senses," 198). During the first day of rain the protagonist recalls a series of images of the past, of those hot days in August when it was not raining like this. At the end of this imagery the narrator demonstrates a second sign of some still inexplicable change: "Súbitamente me sentí sobrecogida por una agobiadora tristeza," (99)

("Suddenly I felt overcome by an overwhelming sadness," 199). Nevertheless, this sensation is not explained.

By the next day, Monday, the protagonist is more explicit about changes in both the nature of the rain and her mental state. There seems to be an intuitive link between the two: "Pero entonces parecía como si estuviera lloviendo de otro modo, porque algo distinto y amargo occurría en mi corazón," (99) ("But now it seemed to be raining in another way, because something different and bitter was going in my heart," 199–200). This link is expressed as a direct physical one by Tuesday, although the reader still interprets it as metaphorical: "Al atardecer del martes el agua apretaba y dolía como una mortaja en el corazón" (99) ("At sundown on Tuesday the water tightened and hurt, like a shroud over the heart," 200).

This same day there is a significant change in the everyday life, a notable breakdown in rational order. This day they lose track of the most regular of all daily routines, the order of meals. The narrator even states that from that moment they quit thinking ("dejamos de pensar"). The situation is relatively similar on Wednesday, in which there is total "disorder" in the household.

The final step in this bizarre series of changes in the physical and mental world of the protagonist occurs on Thursday. On the one hand, the protagonist loses all sense of time and space, a fact which is stated in a most matter-of-fact manner: "Al amanecer del jueves cesaron los olores, se perdió el sentido de las distancias. La noción del tiempo, trastornada desde el día anterior, desapareció por completo" (102) ("At dawn on Thursday the smells stopped, the sense of distance was lost. The notion of time, upset since the day before, disappeared completely," 205). The physical world has been transformed in such a way that even human bodies are "cuerpos adiposos e improbables que se movían en el tremedal del invierno" (103) ("adipose and improbable bodies that moved in the marsh of winter," 205). The narrator somehow relates the transformation of the physical world to her own mental state when she states that a "zone" of her consciousness still had not totally awakened. This statement seems contradictory: if she is indeed communicating all these perceptions of the world around her, how is it possible that she is not totally awake?

The end of the story resolves this ambiguous situation. The surprising revelation that the protagonist is dead makes the flexibility

of the physical world at least understandable. It is the final step in
the creation of a physical world that escapes rational explanation.

The use of a first-person narrator is key to the creation of the
sense of disintegration that pervades the story. The natural limi-
tations of a narrator within the story who is also the protagonist
create the instabilities that are key elements of the story. The basic
narrative situation is that a first-person narrator tells the story in
retrospective fashion, referring to the events exclusively in the past
tense. Vargas Llosa has found a subtle distinction that systematically
marks this narrative mode: García Márquez employs a first-person
plural ("nosotros") when the narrator refers to the immediate situation—the weather—and a first-person singular ("yo") when the
narrator evokes the past.[14] On the one hand, the very narrative
system consequently undermines a sense of organic homogeneous
unity. The perspective of the story, like the substance of the fictional
world, is in flux. Ideology and narrative point of view thus are
joined in this experience of disintegration. The dual perspective also
contributes to the narrator's credibility in at least two ways. This
credibility creates for the reader a sense that there are indeed changes
in the physical world, rather than, for example, exclusively a case
of progressive mental breakdown on the part of the narrator or an
inability to perceive the world normally. The first vehicle for the
creation of this credibility is the description of the exterior world
not as a vision interpreted personally by her, but a view perceived
by others as well. For example, at the beginning of the story, the
narrator *and* her stepmother are observing the rain and rejoicing
about it. The constant references to this weather from the perspective
of "we" emphasizes changes in the exterior world rather than just
one person's perception of it.

The use of the first-person singular acquires credibility because
it does not rely on immediate perception either, but rather past
events other than the rain. Thus, the memories of those hot days
in August are in the first-person singular; so is the noting of her
pregnancy.

"Monologue of Isabel Watching It Rain in Macondo" can be seen
as a transition between the initial stories of the 1948–52 period
and the later fiction of Macondo. As in the initial stories, García
Márquez is visibly interested in placing into question traditional
concepts of space and time and tends to privilege the use of the
language of "time" as part of his discourse. The progressive flow of

the rain eventually creates that "other reality" to which García Márquez also aspired in the earlier stories. Once again, this special state is a kind of inexplicable stage between life and death. This story marks a significant beginning because it is the first story of Macondo. The surprise at the end marks the use of at least one traditional narrative technique—suspense. The later fiction of Macondo will embody both the most inventive and traditional narrative techniques. Perhaps most importantly, García Márquez has made an enormous step in the fictionalization of a reader. Any reader will be immediately intrigued—indeed, attracted—by such items as this curious weather that becomes a physical substance. It is quite an improvement over the pretentiously confusing beginnings of the earlier stories. The reader in "Monologue of Isabel Watching It Rain in Macondo" plays an attractive role as participant experiencing this strange reality, all the way to the intriguing discovery of the narrator's situation at the end.

The real reader of the "Tale of a Castaway" was technically defined more than in any of his previous stories. This specified recipient of the text is a reader of newspapers. The story belongs to a genre located somewhere in the realm of creative journalism, or journalistic fiction. Some critics mention the story briefly with reference to García Márquez's writing; none includes it as an integral part of his short fiction. This oversight is paradoxical because of the recognized fact that the development of García Márquez's writing is closely tied to his journalistic career. In addition, it functions as a revealing element with respect to García Márquez's position regarding artistic creation and Colombian society.

The "Tale of a Castaway" was published originally as fourteen serialized articles in Bogotá's newspaper *El Espectador*. It reconstructed the story of a real person, Luis Alejandro Velasco, a twenty-year-old sailor who was shipwrecked while aboard the Colombian ship *Caldas* in February 1955. García Márquez interviewed him extensively to acquire his basic anecdotal material. The result was a superb adventure story.

The fourteen anecdotes tell Velasco's story from his last days in Mobile, Alabama, before the ship's departure, through the ten days he spent on a raft, and, at the end, his reception in Colombia as a hero. At the beginning of the story, Velasco and his companions of the *Caldas* had spent eight months in Mobile where the naval ship was being repaired. In their last few days of furlough, they spend their time as typical sailors: drinking at their favorite bar (in this case, Joe Palooka's) and occasionally becoming involved in a barroom scuffle. Velasco takes his American girlfriend, Mary Address, to the movies. The sailors depart, despite the protagonist's premonition that the trip would be dangerous, and the ship sinks in a storm. Velasco is the only survivor. During the ten days alone on a raft he suffers a variety of terrors: the memories of his dead friends; the threat of death, a real possibility because of sharks; the hope of being rescued by an airplane, which dissipates when the plane never returns; the desperate attempt to stay alive by eating raw fish caught with his bare hands.

The story is related in first-person by Velasco, in retrospection. It is a somewhat special narrative situation: a first-person narrator of historical existence (and even alive at the time of the publication of the story) is fictionalized by a writer with an identity as both a journalist and fiction writer. The narrator's memory is meticulous. One can safely affirm that Velasco and his tale are fictionalized because the story is predominantly a creation of García Márquez the fiction writer, only disguised, at best, as García Márquez the journalist. Within the broad outline of a basically "true" story, García Márquez adroitly manipulates the anecdote to maintain a level of suspense, drama, and human interest necessary for a newspaper series. In short, entertainment was the highest priority, not historical accuracy.

The story of a man floating adrift at sea has considerable potential for repetition and boredom. García Márquez avoids both by carefully including a noteworthy anecdote each day—the first day it is the terror of the first night, followed by the day the airplane passes without seeing him, a hallucination, and the arrival of the sharks. What could be identified as both exterior and interior threats maintain the suspense for the reader, manipulating reader interest by some type of particularly dramatic revelation at the end of each chapter. The exterior threat is the terror of death. This is the long-term threat that seems to await Velasco in his condition as shipwreck. The immediate threat, often evoked, is represented by the sharks that appear regularly. The interior threat is embodied in the profound solitude and occasional hallucinations that could destroy him psychologically. This threat is evoked even after he seems to have been saved: as he swims to the shore where he has fixed his eyes on some coconut trees, he suffers a flash of terror with the realization that perhaps he is swimming to a hallucination.

The dramatic touches occasionally border on melodrama. The author portrays all the characters with great care at the beginning of the story, focusing on making them the common, everyday types with whom any newspaper reader can associate. The romance with Mary Address serves this humanizing function for Velasco, and is masterfully evoked later when Velasco suddenly remembers Mary on the eighth day at sea (chapter 9). After his return, he is informed of the romantic coincidence that Mary was holding a mass that very same day to put his soul to rest. Similarly, Velasco humanizes one colleague, Sabogal, carefully noting that his wife and six children would be waiting for him in Cartagena.

Seen within the context of García Márquez's total fiction, the story is notably his and not Velasco's. The writer uses Velasco's heroic venture as material for articulating one of his constant literary preoccupations, conventional concepts of time and space. As such, Velasco suffers from the type of experience with reality that many of García Márquez's characters, even from the 1948–52 period, had perceived. By the fourth day at sea the protagonist suffers from a confusion of time: "Al cuarto día ya no estaba muy seguro de mis cuentas en relación con los días que llevaba de estar en la balsa. ¿Eran tres? ¿Eran cuatro? ¿Eran cinco?"[15] ("By the fourth day I wasn't sure of my count as far as the number of days I had been in the raft. Was it three? Four? Five?"). His relationship to reality is more acutely altered by the ninth day: "Hay un instante en que ya no se siente el dolor. La sensibilidad desaparece ye la razón empieza a embotarse hasta cuando se pierde la noción del tiempo y del espacio" (75–76) ("There is an instant in which one no longer feels the pain. Sensibility disappears and reason starts to get dull until one loses all sense of time and space").

The solitude that is ubiquitous in García Márquez's fiction of Macondo is also important in this story. Once his companions have drowned, the next section (in chapter 3) is titled "Solo" ("Alone"), and the most constant emotion he feels in the remainder of the story is solitude. There is a subtle linguistic shift early in the story which establishes solitude as central: the narrator describes his state as follows: "mi tercer día de soledad en el mar" (46) ("the third day of my solitude in the sea"). The normal word in this phrase should be "naufragio" ("shipwreck") instead of "soledad" ("solitude"), but the narrator has shifted from his physical state (as "naufragio") to his psychic one (as "soledad").

The "Tale of a Castaway" is fundamentally an entertainment. García Márquez considers himself a political person and desires to be seen as a political writer. His declarations about Latin American politics and reality are abundant and well known even by the nonspecialist (see chapter 8). This fact has led many critics to insist upon finding social symbolism in literally everything García Márquez writes. García Márquez himself probably insists so much about his politics for the benefit of those readers and critics at the other end of the spectrum—those who fail to understand the profound social function of works so clearly historical and political as *One Hundred Years of Solitude* and *The Autumn of the Patriarch*. The "Tale of a Castaway" occupies a curious position with respect to this question. García Márquez himself admits that the story was written for *El Espectador* with the express purpose of entertainment. [16] The censorship of a military government, in effect, required the opposition newspaper, *El Espectador,* to seek the political neutrality of entertainment. Read as fourteen stories about a heroic Colombian sailor, García Márquez's account can be seen as nothing other than the most neutral of such entertainment. When it was published later as a book, however, in 1970, García Márquez converted it into an ideologeme, a socially symbolic act. [17] He did this by including a type of prologue to the book ("Historia de mi historia") which gives it a political content of which even García Márquez was unaware when he originally wrote the story. The political and moral charge, which García Márquez admits he had never suspected when he wrote the story, came forth when it was revealed that the government ship was carrying contraband, the overload and not a storm being the real cause of the eight sailors' demise. A few months after this scandalous revelation, *El Espectador* was closed by the government. García Márquez's republication of the story in 1970 with the prologue makes it the political act that it was not in 1955.

García Márquez's initial discovery of such writers as Kafka, Borges, and Faulkner in the 1940s had inspired a frontal attack on traditional concepts of reality. His work on *Leafstorm,* actually written in the early 1950s well before this tale, reflects a concern for Colombia's concrete historical reality. He obviously felt a need to deal with both abstract and concrete reality. The "Tale of a Castaway" in a certain way freed García Márquez momentarily from this dilemma and concerns about concrete reality in particular: the only real priority was entertainment. García Márquez used this opportunity just to tell a good story, a skill he will continue to use adroitly no matter what the nature of the fictional world or social context.

Leafstorm (1955)

The first novel of Macondo was *Leafstorm*. Most of the action takes place in Macondo from 1903 to 1928; one critic has pointed out correctly that a more exact description sets the time from Macondo's foundation to 1928.[18] The word "action" is also misleading—it is more a novel of atmosphere than events. Events are blurred by a sequence and lack of explanation that quite often make their rational understanding secondary to their effects. All the characters in "Monologue of Isabel Watching It Rain in Macondo" are present in this novel. Thus, the short story is modified by a reading of this novel, just as this novel is modified by a reading of *One Hundred Years of Solitude*. All of the fiction of Macondo functions in this manner. *Leafstorm* was written in 1950–51, and "Monologue of Isabel Watching It Rain in Macondo" was a product of the same rough draft that produced the novel.[19]

The story is of Macondo; the focus lies primarily on four characters: three persons in a family who narrate and a doctor whose wake is the basic circumstance of the novel. The work consists of twenty-nine segments, ranging in length from about three to five pages. After an initial segment which is narrated from a collective "we" point of view, the story changes to the first of three narrators in the family, a ten-year-old boy. The boy, at the wake, relates his thoughts and perceptions of the moment. The other voices are the boy's mother, Isabel, and his grandfather.

The most important event to take place in this small town during this quarter century is the arrival and departure of the "leafstorm"— the people and unbridled progress associated with an American banana company. The once innocent and rural town becomes a center for the chaos and corruption often linked with modernity. The "banana boom" resulted in a swift, but artificial prosperity that produced scenes like parties where money was burned in celebrations. The nouveau riche of the teens, along with the workers that followed them, are resented by the town's original founders. The grandfather, for example, belongs to this group of the older families, the historical aristocracy, that precedes the arrival of the company and resents the anonymous mass of people associated with it.

A reconstructed chronology of the events reveals the arrival of many of the traditional families near the end of the nineteenth century. There is a reference to the grandfather's involvement in a civil war in 1885. Later, in 1903, Colonel Aureliano Buendía is a commander of the area. This is the year the colonel writes a letter of presentation on behalf of the doctor, who is then accepted by Isabel's father as a guest in his house. He stays eight years. The period of most ebullient prosperity was about 1915. There is textual evidence that the company had left Macondo by 1918; the last ten years of the novel's history are the period of postboom decadence.

The reader also gains some awareness of what Macondo is like in 1928. It is drained and tired, languishing in a nostalgia for a distant past and disdain for the recent history of what has been identified as the leafstorm. An exact moment in the present of 1928 is detailed: it is 2:30 in the afternoon, and an image of a woman evokes the atmosphere of this worn-out town: "I think about Senora Rebecca, thin and looking like parchment, with the touch of a family ghost in her look and dress, sitting beside her electric fan, her face shaded by the screens in her windows."[20] The other scenes evoked at 2:30 by Isabel are equally depressing: a cripple watches a pair of lovers say goodbye to each other at the train station, and we see him turning a deserted corner; the mail arrives delivered by a mule cloaked in a cloud of dust; the town priest sits dozing and belches.

When asked in 1982 what he thought about the young writer who authored his first novel, García Márquez explained that he views him with "a little compassion, because he wrote it quickly, thinking that he wasn't going to write anything else in his life, that that was his only opportunity, and so he tried to put into that book everything learned by then. Especially techniques and literary tricks taken from the American and English novels that he was reading."[21] Even without being aware of García Márquez's direct Faulknerian connection, the techniques most apparently adopted from foreign authors are the use of the structure and point of view from *As I Lay Dying*. Concerned with some critics' contention that *Leafstorm* is little more than a Spanish version of this Faulkner novel, García Márquez maintains, with the same retrospection of twenty-seven years since the publication of the first novel: "It isn't exactly the same [as *As I Lay Dying*]. I utilize three perfectly identifiable points of view without giving them names: that of an old man, a boy and a woman. If you look carefully, *Leafstorm* has the same technique (points of view organized around a dead person) as *The Autumn of the Patriarch*. Only that in *Leafstorm* I didn't dare let myself loose, the monologues are rigorously systematized."[22]

Technically speaking, the novel includes not three, but four basic points of view. These are the voices of a collective "we" in the novel's first section, followed by the three first-person singular points of view. Each of these four voices has a different function. The collective "we" of the first section is a lyrical, poetic discourse with a broad, historical framework. The lyrical quality of the language and broadness of the historical context are effects that García Márquez would have difficulty evoking in the interior monologues.

"Suddenly, as if a whirlwind had set down in the center of town, the banana company arrived, pursued by the leafstorm." (9). This opening line of the novel establishes its central metaphor, the leafstorm. It also refers to the banana company, without giving it a name or other background information. This procedure has two effects. First it makes the situation portrayed general enough to be appreciated as a universal problem, rather than only a specific historical situation such as, for example, the relationship between the United Fruit Company and its workers. Second, by not naming a specific banana company or place, García Márquez praises his fictionalized reader, a praise established by the implicit understanding between author and reader that this is at least an historical pattern recognizable by the informed reader of Latin American fiction.

The remainder of this first section describes the ugliness of a modernity imposed from the outside. There are numerous references to the "rubble" that has arrived, the objects and persons associated with the modernity in this novel. They include hospitals, amusement parlors, and electric plants. The people that come to this town are described as the "dregs" of society because they include persons of the type who arrive unmarried and who do not fit into Macondo's traditional society: their rapid purchasing of houses and equally quick acquisition of military titles does not lead to acceptance in society.

Just who is this established society of Macondo? Its voice is the collective "we" of this first section:

Even the dregs of the cities' sad love came to *us* in the whirlwind and
built small wooden houses where at first a corner and a half-cot were a
dismal home for one night, and then a noisy clandestine street, and then
a whole inner village of tolerance within the town. (10; my italics)

Here it is the group that lived in the town before the institution-
alization of prostitution in the town. The condemnation by the "we"
has a moral overtone.

In addition to their moral opposition to the changes brought by
the newcomers, the voice of the "we" feels it has been replaced or
pushed aside by them. The narrator states: "the first of us came to
be the last; we were the outsiders, the newcomers" (10). This is the
only section of the novel with this "we" voice.

In the next four sections the reader finds three different narrative
voices. These include two segments narrated by the boy, one by his
mother, and one by the grandfather. Each is a first-person singular
narrative. Their respective functions in the text, however, vary considerably. Of the three narrators, the boy's narration inscribes as its
temporal and spatial boundaries the most limited framework. He
tends to limit his focus to his immediate thoughts and feelings while
sitting at the doctor's wake. Even references to a past involve the
immediate past of the day at the wake. The section begins as follows:
"I've seen a corpse for the first time. It's Wednesday but I feel as
if it were Sunday because I didn't go to school and they dressed me
up in a green corduroy suit that's tight in some places" (15). The
boy's narration is controlled by the verb "to see." The past temporal
reference to having been dressed up in a suit is used only to indicate
how uncomfortable he feels at the present moment. The present
tense of "to feel" is also constant throughout the boy's narration.
In the fourth paragraph seven of its nine sentences begin with the
phrase "I can see . . . ," emphasizing the immediacy of experience
for the narrator and reader. The total experience of the first section
communicates the reaction of a young boy to his first wake and
reveals the basic situation, the presence of the three narrators and
four Guajiro Indians at the wake.

The boy's second narration functions at the same level of information communicated to the reader. Its references to the past are
limited to what the boy has experienced doing Wednesday. Thoughts
and feelings of the moment, however, dominate the section. The
last paragraph consists of a series of sentences that enumerate what

the child *sees:* the town, his house, Pepe, a boy, the house next door.

The mother's narration seems quite similar, being another first-person view of the events at hand. The information it communicates, however, is quite different: the boy's vision is limited to a very immediate reality; the mother expands reality to widen the boundaries of the fictionalized world. Like the boy, she reacts to the immediate situation of the wake. The boy's sense of the past is limited to the events prior to the wake. The mother refers to a past that stretches back some twenty-five years, when the doctor arrived at their home. In her first narration she also refers to the time when Meme, the doctor's concubine, had disappeared some eleven years before. Less limited by time than her son, the mother defines her boundaries not by time, but by space. Her basic frame of reference is a small group of characters that define a small space in Macondo— those persons in her immediate physical presence, such as her family, the doctor, and Meme. Her role as narrator is thus determined by her traditional role as mother: her narration, like her life, is limited to a small group of persons within her social realm.

The grandfather, both as narrator and element in this hierarchical society, is the voice of maximum authority. He provides both synchronic and diachronic perspectives on Macondo. In the first chapter it is *he* who for the first time in the novel provides some explanation for why the doctor is so hated: he had refused the town's demand for medical attention in a crisis situation. It is appropriate that the grandfather provide this bit of information because it is he who functions, in effect, as the town's historian: the boy tells his own story, the mother tells the family's story, and the grandfather tells the town's story. As the voice of authority in the text, he also occupies the largest textual space in the novel: he has twelve monologues, in comparison to the mother's ten and the son's six.

García Márquez attains several effects with this use of narrative point of view. The effect of the three types of narration is different from novels that use the juxtaposition of small fragments. This novel moves the reader back into time and even more into the underlying reality of the situation.[23] The move in time is effected primarily by the grandfather and secondarily by the mother; the moved into the underlying or subjective reality of the situation is effected primarily by the boy and secondarily by the mother.

Leafstorm represents García Márquez's first novelistic attempt at
creating an "other reality," beyond the bounds of normal, objective
perception. In some of the early stories this "other reality" involved
strange states of existence somehow between life and death. There
is a certain similarity in the procedure here: a death serves as the
point of departure to probe the underlying reality of the town.
Several factors create a fictional world which does not adhere to the
cause and effect relationships of empirical reality. In some cases
effects are simply evident before causes. For example, several of the
mother's references to the family situation are only effects; the grandfather's explanation of the historical background provides the causes.
In other, more entertaining cases, however, the effects are devoid
of causes. The doctor requests grass to eat for dinner. The text offers
no explanation for this absurd demand, nor does any underlying
symbolic scheme account for it. Likewise, a priest reads from the
Bristal Almanac. It is a curious world, sometimes better enjoyed in
all its humorous splendor than rationally explained.

The language that García Márquez uses to describe the objects
and emotions of this fictional world also contributes to the spe-
cialness of its reality. Combining "objects" and "emotions" might
appear to be incongruous, but not in this novel. García Márquez
attempts to create a special reality by attacking the limits which
normally distinguish objects from abstractions. The following passage demonstrates how García Márquez handles the normally abstract notion of time:

But the new movement is frustrated, my father comes into the room and
the two times are reconciled; the two halves become adjusted, consolidated,
and Senora Rebecca's clock realizes that it's been caught between the child's
parsimony and the widow's impatience, and then it yawns, confused, dives
into the prodigious quiet of the moment and comes out afterward dripping
with liquid time, with exact and rectified time. . . . (70–71)

First, the narrator personifies a time caught between two emotions,
a personified clock caught between parsimony and impatience. Then
time becomes an object which drips as liquid. Earlier in this same
segment, narrated by Isabel, sleep, reality, and a thread are used
in a surprising juxtaposition: "And then they go back to huddling
in the corner, splicing sleep to reality . . . weaving the whispering
as if it were an immense flat surface of thread stitched in common

by all the women in town" (67). At times the young writer's interest in creating special effects with language is betrayed by a direct explanation of the special quality of the reality. For example, the boy observes that when the window is open things become visible, but consolidated in their "strange unrealness" (20). When the grandfather describes the scene of the first dinner with the newly arrived doctor, he states: "Never before had I seen in my house an environment more loaded with unreality" (65). In cases like this, the professional uses of metaphor involving the abstract and concrete give way to the amateur still anxious to create this "other reality." The instances of such flaws are rare.

There are numerous ways of describing the nature of this other reality in this particular novel and in García Márquez's fiction in general. It can be called a mythic vision of reality. One critic has demonstrated that time conceived as prolonged or continuous present is one category that shows the configuration of myth in this novel. [24] The breakdown of the traditional concept of a chronological, flowing time implies a mythic vision. The four subcategories of the continuous present in this novel are (1) the half-hour duration of the novel, (2) a historical past spanning a period of twenty-five years (the central focus 1903–28), (3) a more imprecise past dating to the founding of Macondo, and (4) the subjective, psychological time of the three narrators who remember the past. [25] As has been pointed out, each of these three conceives a distinctly different past. Still another way of viewing the singularity of the reality in this novel is suggested by what John S. Brushwood identifies as transcendent regionalism. [26] This critic points out that even writers operating on a clearly delineated regional base, such as Faulkner, utilize certain narrative techniques to create an experience for the reader which transcends regional or national boundaries, in effect, a universal experience. The comparison with Faulkner in this case, of course, is more than coincidence (see chapter 1).

The different visions of reality also imply a variety of discourse. As such, *Leafstorm* represented García Márquez's most prolific creation of a world of heteroglossia, a rich incorporation of different languages. In this sense it was García Márquez's most ambitious project up to 1955. The novel's opening section embodies both traditional literary discourse and an historical discourse: the metaphor of the "leafstorm" announces the literary language, and the placement of the words "Macondo, 1909" at the very end of this section is an incorporation of ostensibly historical language. The grandfather's narration represents the continuity of this historical context. There is a layer of what might be identified as the language of transcendent regionalism. Here García Márquez uses a language which itself seems to strive for the universality of the transcendent regionalist tradition in Spanish American literature. For example, the mother claims that there was a "lot of incredible legend" in what one character says (44). These suggestions of legend in the language itself create a mythical level of reality. The abstract language that appropriates objects and the objectification of abstractions is still another level of incorporation of different languages in this dialogic text.

The different types of language in this novel expose ideology as the fabric of textual organization. In addition to the conflicts evident between Macondo's inhabitants and modernity that the reader observes in the novel's events, the language embodies a hierarchical, at times even medieval world. One aspect of the hierarchical order is the grandfather's role as maximum authority as a narrative voice. In the male-dominated society, the woman functions as an accessory, which is the mother's role in this novel. She describes overhearing conversations between her father and a character named Martín; later her marriage with Martín was arranged without her even having established a superficial friendship with him. The language of this medieval world is of mysterious forces and prophecies. The mother's description of her world employs this language:

It wasn't I who arranged things in my own home, but some other mysterious force, one which decided the course of our existence and of which we were nothing but docile and insignificant instruments. Everything seemed to obey the natural and linked fulfillment of a prophecy. (107)

The narrator also employs a biblical language at times. The English translation loses some of the biblical overtones in the grandfather's description of the initial building of Macondo. With biblical repetition, it has traces of the original creation: "Y lo hicieron. Y aguardaron en él los materiales del templo en construcción."[27] Here the repetition works well, particularly when associated with the church that is mentioned in the sentence. The published English translation unfortunately does not offer the repetition: "Which they did. Inside they kept the materials for the construction of the church"

(50). (A free translation that might retain the flavor would be: "And it came to pass. And therein kept they the materials whereof the temple should be built.")

Leafstorm can be seen as a symbolic act that attempts to harmonize elements that are ideologically heterogeneous. The medieval, nascent capitalist, and foreign capitalist societies are placed in uncomfortable juxtaposition. The characters, most importantly the three narrators, articulate language that communicates this heterogeneity. The novel portrays a world in disintegration; it is a society in decay, rich in the layers of language that have persisted as society has decayed. The central figure of the novel, the doctor, functions as a metaphor for this society. His physical and moral rot, in addition to his alienation from Macondo's society, reflect the corruption and weaknesses of Macondo.[28]

As García Márquez's initial novel-length voyage into the land of Macondo, *Leafstorm* is a remarkably successful venture in the creation of an "other reality." This success is due to the ability to fictionalize a reader who experiences a myth, rather than having to have it explained. The intricacies of the structure and the characters are a process discovered by the reader, who assumes a necessarily active role in reconstructing a Macondo in a present state of disintegration. Both a specifically Colombian social reality and a universal experience are important aspects of this book. The short stories and two short novels that immediately follow *Leafstorm* represent a move toward the former, a reflection on Colombian and Latin-American society.

Chapter Three
The Middle Years (1956–62)

Introduction: García Márquez,
La Violencia, and Social Literature

Within his Colombian context, García Márquez's writing career up to 1955 was exceptional—a very rare anomaly. During the early years he was conscientiously laboring over the type of imaginative literature in which only he and his small group of friends of the Group of Barranquilla were interested. The publication of *Leafstorm* was the first of three major novels written by writers from the coast (see chapter 1). None of these three writers would be associated with socialist realism by even the most insistent Marxist. Even the social reality which *Leafstorm* does concern, the banana production, makes it anomolous in Colombia: Colombia's principal agricultural base since the late nineteenth century has been coffee, not bananas. [1] The exceptionality of a Colombian book, published in 1955, with Faulknerian and mythical overtones, taking place in the banana producing zone, can be appreciated by placing García Márquez briefly in the Latin American and Colombian literary scenario. On the one hand, the rise of the New Novel in Spanish America in the late 1940s, the publication of Borges's *Ficciones* during the same period, and the popularization of Faulkner throughout the Hispanic world makes García Márquez's interests seem totally natural. On the other hand, Spanish America, and Colombia in particular, also have a venerable tradition of social literature of the realist vein. In the hemispheric context, the appearance of *Leafstorm* is unexceptional; in the Colombian tradition, however, it ushers in the New Novel.

The overwhelmingly dominant preoccupation of virtually all Colombian writers during the 1950s was the civil was between Liberals and Conservatives, *la violencia.* Documentary-type accounts of the brute violence and stories of individual and family tragedy abound in Colombian fiction of the period and thereafter. The fiction during this period of the Colombians José A. Osorio Lizarazo, Eduardo Caballero Calderón, and Manuel Zapata Olivella, to name a few prominent examples, was predominantly concerned with the portrayal of moral problems within their social contexts rather than with the inventive aspects of fiction.[2]

Paradoxically, it was during the period that García Márquez was most distanced from Colombia that he became most intimately involved with its specific social realities in his fiction. It was during his stay outside Colombia in the middle to late 1950s that he wrote most of the stories later published as *Big Mama's Funeral* and two short novels, *No One Writes to the Colonel* and *In Evil Hour*. In 1970 García Márquez explained this move as follows: "I decided to approach the reality of the moment in Colombia and I wrote *No One Writes to the Colonel* and *In Evil Hour*."[3] Twelve years later he provided a more precise description of the fiction to this period: *"No One Writes to the Colonel* and *Big Mama's Funeral* are books inspired in Colombia's reality and their rationalist structure is determined by the nature of the theme. I don't regret having written them, but they constitute a type of premeditated literature that offers a somewhat static and exclusive view of reality."[4] With these three books García Márquez fictionalizes the political and human reality of Colombia—its institutions and the effects of its civil war. He also continues to develop some of his already established literary preoccupations and ambitions.

Big Mama's Funeral (1962)

The first line of the title story brings to García Márquez's fiction a very important element previously lacking in his writing: hyperbolic humor. It begins as follows:

Esta es, incrédulos del mundo entero, la verídica historia de la Mamá Grande, soberana absoluta del reino de Macondo, que vivió en función de dominio durante 92 años y murió en olor de santidad un martes del septiembre pasado, y a cuyos funerales vino el Sumo Pontífice.[5]

This is, for all the world's unbelievers, the true account of Big Mama, absolute sovereign of the Kingdom of Macondo, who lived for ninety-two years, and died in the odor of sanctity one Tuesday last September, and whose funeral was attended by the Pope.[6]

There is a considerable use of such humor in this story. The volume is not uniformly humorous hyperbole, although it does contain some humor and other elements new to the author's fictional world. Two stories of this type are "Balthazar's Marvelous Afternoon" and "One Day After Saturday." Some of the stories represent a further development of the literature of Macondo, which involved not only locating the stories there, but also developing characters who would regularly appear in the Macondo fiction. This is one way that García Márquez's fiction is modified by reading: just as the reader's experience of "Monologue of Isabel Watching It Rain" is changed after reading *Leafstorm,* the experience of *One Hundred Years of Solitude* will be changed after gaining an awareness of these stories. Some of these stories, such as "One of These Days" and "Montiel's Widow," deal with *la violencia.*

"Big Mama's Funeral," as the title and first line suggest, tells the story of the funeral for this most prodigious woman. The narrator explains at the beginning that, now that all the commotion has calmed down, he will tell the true story of the events relating to her funeral, before the historians have time to arrive on the scene. It all began, according to the narrator, some fourteen weeks before the story's temporal present, when the dying Big Mama demanded that she be placed on her rocking chair and taken upstairs in order to make her final requests. The priest stays in her room permanently because he is so obese that it takes ten men to carry him up to Big Mama's room and thus it would require too much work for him to be taken down only to return upon her death. Approximately the first half of the story relates more details concerning the death scene and the immediate surroundings. No one in the town, Macondo, is indifferent to the prospect of the death of a member of the distinguished family that had been among the town's original founders. Her power is described in the hyperbolically humorous proportions that will later be evoked in the general's request for absolute and total power in *The Autumn of the Patriarch.* For example, everyone believes that she is the owner of all water, all the rain and future rains, the neighborhood streets, the telegraph poles, and rights over all lives. None of Macondo's inhabitants had ever thought that she might be mortal.

When the final moment does come, it is an event of the most enormous magnitude. During this moment, Big Mama gives her last instructions. First, she lists all her property before two witnesses.

She takes three hours to list her possessions. Finished with this laborious task, she lists what she calls her "bienes morales," or "moral goods," which she defines as such things as the underground riches, the territorial waters, the colors of the flag, national sovereignty, the traditional parties, human rights, and civil liberty. The list continues with numerous other items that are part of her "moral goods." Before finishing this list, she suddenly expires.

Her death has immediate impact on the entire nation: the newspapers carry her picture as a twenty year old and are filled with articles about her illustrious life. The capital enters a period of mourning; even the president finds his ministers dressed for mourning. Sensing the national emotion over the funeral, the president declares nine days of official national mourning. After numerous manipulations of the constitution, the politicians and bureaucrats arrange for the president to be able to leave the capital for the funeral. Even the pope, impressed by Big Mama's picture in the newspaper, prepares for his sojourn to the funeral. Despite the suffering involved in the canoe trip to Macondo, the pope makes the sacrifices necessary for this important ritual. He is joined by representatives from all levels of the institutional bureaucracy, even the numerous beauty queens of Colombia's different festivals. Both the pope and these Colombian citizens can now breathe a sigh of relief: the reign of Big Mama's power on earth has ended.

The outstanding feature of the story is its hyperbolic humor, particularly within the context of García Márquez's previous writing. The brief flashes of humor evident in *Leafstorm* are abundant in "Big Mama's Funeral." The hyperbole functions on various levels. The characterization of Big Mama, with her enormous proportions, is an exercise in exaggeration in itself. Her entire life is one of excesses. On another level, the story's plot, which is placed into motion after her death approximately midway through the story, is hyperbole. It is humorous because of the incongruity between Macondo's backward simplicity and the national and international importance placed on the death of its matriarch. At this level García Márquez carries out his satire of traditional Colombian society: the Colombian reader, for example, will recognize the satire involved in enumerating *nine* different beauty queens who pass by Big Mama's cadaver. Probably no country in the world sponsors more beauty contests than Colombia.

Hyperbole is most commonly associated with language itself, and this is another level of its function in this story. Telling the story here is the elaborate enumeration of words for the sake of words, in which the narrator explains in the second paragraph that the entire nation has calmed down, including "the bagpipers of San Jacinto, the smugglers of Guajira, the rice planters of Sinú, the prostitutes of Caucamayal, the wizards of Sierpe, and the banana workers of Aracataca" (153). The detail of the enumeration of Big Mama's power is equally humorous. The hyperbolic language is a constant source of humor in the story.

The language in the story is what Bakhtin would call a rich dialogue, in this case a variety of mostly institutional languages. García Márquez incorporates these different languages as a way of ridiculing the nation's basic institutions. The lengthy enumeration of all the beauty queens cited above is a satire of a certain type of ceremonious language and a ridicule of the institution of beauty pageants. The most elaborate and successful use of heteroglossia in the story appears, significantly enough, as a type of linguistic culmination right before Big Mama's death. Here García Márquez places all the rich baggage of the worn-out clichés of the traditional institutions, particularly the political ones. This appears as the list of Big Mama's "invisible" belongings, an extensive paragraph of some forty items. Most of them are political clichés, such as "national sovereignty," "the rights of man," "civil rights," "the right of appeal," "free elections," "huge demonstrations," and "the free but responsible press." It is only appropriate that after this linguistic outburst Big Mama dies: the heteroglossia has reached a point of maximum and exhausted expression.

The reduction of the story line to a basic description of what happens in the story would produce the following nuclear sentence: "The protagonist dies."[7] Seen in this fashion, the story can be divided easily into two parts: a first part that precedes her death and a second part which focuses on the period immediately following the death, the funeral. The formulation of the nuclear sentence in this way, however, excludes the element of language that is so essential to the total experience of this story. A revealing sentence is the following formulation: "A protagonist dictates." This sentence captures the essence of the story in several ways. First, it is notable that the verb "to dictate" appears constantly in association with Big Mama, although often under different guises, such as "to order," "to demand," or "to ask for." In any case, Big Mama functions in the story as the person who dictates or demands. After the narrator's two-paragraph introduction, Big Mama's story begins with her giving orders: "Fourteen weeks ago . . . , Big Mama ordered . . ." (153). The narrator commonly employs the verb "pedir" ("to ask for") with Big Mama. When she makes the final list of all her belongings, it is notable that her penultimate act is to "dictate" ("dictated to the notary this list of her invisible estate," 137). Her final act too is *to emit,* appropriately enough, although it is her most vulgar final "dictation": "Big Mama emitted a loud belch and expired," (161).

In her privileged position as the one who dictates, Big Mama exercises maximum authority in a traditional and hierarchical society. As such, she functions as an ideological sign—an ideologeme—for the extreme limits of power exercised by certain persons in such a society. The structure of society in "Big Mama's Funeral" is a paradigm for certain sectors of Latin America and other parts of the world which are fundamentally medieval in some aspects. This story can thus be read as a burlesque depiction and implied condemnation of the privileged oligarchy. During this period when García Márquez is more overtly concerned with Colombian reality than in his previous work, a story such as this demonstrates a sharp awareness and ability to satirize a type of traditional society.

A more complete consideration of the story reveals what one critic has described as a dual interest in politics and myth.[8] That interest cultivated in the earlier stories in creating some kind of "other reality"—what some critics have identified as myth—is still present in this story, too. On the one hand, the characterization of Big Mama as a truly extraordinary type places her in a legendary realm beyond our everyday reality of cause and effect relationships. Other elements in this story contribute to the creation of myth. One is the use of a particular narrative point of view which focuses on the protagonist from the perspective of the average person on the street.[9] This humble filter facilitates the reader's perception of Big Mama as a very special and even mythic character.

"Big Mama's Funeral" represents considerable progress within García Márquez's fiction in the fictionalization of a reader. It has been demonstrated how his fiction had already been notably improved by the mid-1950s with respect to that fictionalization. David W. Foster has demonstrated that in this particular story there are two readers fictionalized in the text.[10] One such reader, or *narrataire,* is the reader of the official language incorporated into the text. This is the simple and innocent reader implied in the story's first line, that it, the open-mouthed ingenue who will be impressed by the verbal flourishes that accompany the marvelous, extraordinary tale the raconteur is about to unfold.[11] The text fictionalizes this traditional reader who uncritically accepts traditional language and, implicitly, Big Mama's power.

The second reader fictionalized in this story is the element that makes this piece of fiction sophisticated contemporary writing. This reader is critical of the tired, official language: the second fictionalized reader of García Márquez's story is the reader who is supposed to be able to gauge the distance between official history, folk legend, and demythifying literature.[12] This more sophisticated second reader rejects both certain languages and the first reader who reads such languages literally. Foster explains how this second reader rejects the first through five processes: exaggeration, incredible circumstance, remote or unusual practices, ironic language, and pejorative or satiric insinuations.

The humor in "Big Mama's Funeral" thus depends on a certain distanced superiority on the part of the reader. Ong would point out that this story is successful because García Márquez has fictionalized a reader whose role many readers will find appealing to assume. The reader is invited to play a similarly superior role in "Balthazar's Marvelous Afternoon." There the superiority arises directly in relationship to the story's poor protagonist, Balthazar.

Balthazar is an artisan who makes a cage so impressive that he must close down his shop because of the multitude of admirers who come to see his masterpiece. The people in the town consider it the most beautiful object in the world. He is thirty-two years old. He lives with Ursula, who is the same type of figure who will appear in *One Hundred Years of Solitude*. Ursula will serve as the stoic force of common sense and practicality in the novel, in contrast to the dreamer José Arcadio Buendía; in this story she serves the same function in juxtaposition with the impractical Balthazar. She is disgusted with her partner's inattention to his carpentry in favor of two weeks' full-time work on the cage.

The conversation between the pair about the cage is an early character revelation. Her first question about the cage is how much he will charge for it, thus emphasizing her pragmatic mind. When Balthazar humbly indicates that he will probably only ask for thirty pesos, Ursula insists that he demand fifty. She does not base this demand on any qualitative judgment about the cage. Rather, her two points are that it kept him laboring at night (emphasizing its labor value) and its large size (emphasizing quantity over quality). She suggests that for Chepe Montiel such a prize would be insignificant.

Among those impressed with news of the masterpiece is Octavio Giraldo, the town doctor. After studying the cage carefully, he decides to purchase it. Balthazar, however, insists that it is already promised to José Montiel's son, and refuses the doctor's fine monetary offer.

When Balthazar goes to Montiel's home with his cage, the matter of social class becomes more evident. The description of Balthazar entering the town aristocrat's home is telling: "Entonces abrió la puerta de la sala y vio un tumulto, vestido de blanco y acabado de afeitar, con esa expresión de decoroso candor con que los pobres llegan a la casa de los ricos" (69) ("Then she opened the door to the living room and found a crowd in front of the house, and Balthazar with the cage in the middle of the crowd, dressed in white, freshly shaved, with that expression of decorous candor with which the poor approach the houses of the wealthy," 110). The narrator explains the discomfort of the class difference more directly a few lines later: "Pero [Baltazar] nunca se sintió bien entre los ricos" (70) ("But he never felt at ease among the rich," 110). José Montiel shows no interest in the cage, and refuses to purchase the object ordered by his son. Balthazar insists that the child have the cage, giving it to him as a gift rather than leaving him sad and disappointed.

Balthazar arrives at the local bar as a hero. He propagates his own hero status by claiming to have sold the cage to Montiel for sixty pesos. They celebrate the occasion, with Balthazar buying drinks for all. By midnight the usually abstinent carpenter is completely drunk and talking of a fabulous project of constructing a thousand cages at sixty pesos each, and then of building a million. He ends the evening sleeping drunk in the street; women going to 5:00 mass pass by thinking he is dead.

The humor in "Balthazar's Marvelous Afternoon" is achieved with more delicate touches than in the overwhelming and raucous hyperbole of "Big Mama's Funeral." The characterizations of Balthazar and Ursula as opposites are a matter of light humor, rather than devastating satire. García Márquez only begins to use the techniques of exaggeration fully exploited in "Big Mama's Funeral." In his characterization of Montiel, for example, the narrator observes that in his home "nunca se había sentido un olor que no se pudiera vender" (69) ("no one had ever smelled a smell that couldn't be sold," 110). The use of the "nunca" in Spanish ("never") in this sentence is an exaggeration. Later the narrator describes him as "un hombre tan prevenido, que dormía sin ventilador eléctrico para vigilar durante el sueño los rumores de la casa" (70) ("He was such a cautious man that he slept without an electric fan so he could watch over the noises of the house while he slept," 111). Once again, García Márquez pushes the limits of credibility with the use of hyperbolic humor. In these examples one sees traces of the type of humor exploited fully in "Big Mama's Funeral." This particular story tends to create humor of situations: Balthazar's situation with respect to Ursula; his pathetic, but humorous situation with respect to his peers at the end of the story.

The narrative point of view, as in all the stories in this volume, is neutral omniscient. The concern with Colombia's external reality—historical and social—corresponds to the adoption of a more standard, traditional narrative point of view. Unlike the earlier, preprofessional stories, these contain no authorial presence interrupting the flow of the narrative or explaining matters suggested in the story. Rather, García Márquez builds a relationship of confidence between the author and the reader by assigning the reader a privileged position in the text.

The narrator presents two basic perspectives of the events at hand—those represented by Ursula and those represented by Balthazar. The difference between the two views is established from the story's first dialogue:

—Tienes que afeitarte—le dijo Ursula, su mujer—Pareces en capuchino.
—Es malo afeitarse después del almuerzo—dijo Baltazar.

"You have to shave," Ursula, his wife, told him. "You look like a Capuchin."
"It's bad to shave after lunch," said Balthazar. (106)

Ursula is concerned with the practical matter of Balthazar's physical appearance. In his response he demonstrates both his lack of interest in such matters, and a certain comical irrationality: the logical reader questions *why* it is so bad to shave after lunch. This basic dichotomy between Ursula and Balthazar is developed throughout the story. Ursula's initial position concerning the cage is disgust because she feels that her husband had forgotten his work in order to build the cage.

Balthazar's perspective is the artist's. After the initial characterization of Balthazar, Dr. Giraldo provides the first complimentary view of the carpenter as artist: "Esto es una aventura de la imaginación. Hubieras sido un extraordinario arquitecto" (67) ("This is a flight of the imagination. You would have been an extraordinary architect," 108). When the humble Balthazar enters José Montiel's home, he adopts a feeling of the artist's superiority, a momentary "sentimiento de piedad" ("feeling of pity"), thinking about the rich man's problems. The acceptably imaginative cage is transformed in Balthazar's drunk mind into a "fabulous" project of a thousand and then a million such cages, the result of a creator's mind. At the end of the story the fantasy world, Balthazar's view, predominates, when he refuses to abandon "el sueño más feliz su vida" (74) ("the happiest dream of his life," 114).

A third perspective—which rejects the first two as literal interpretations of reality—is implied in the text's total organization. This superior perspective is assumed by the reader fictionalized in this story. One critic has pointed to the "complicity" or "confidential" relationship established between the author and reader in "Balthazar's Marvelous Afternoon."[13] There is a certain complicity involved between the teller and the listener of a joke; a similar relationship between author and reader exists here. The fictionalized reader, rejecting the two basic perspectives, is able to appreciate the humor involved in them. D. W. Foster has shown how the use of the adjective "prodigiosa" ("prodigious") is the first step in the creation of this complicity.[14] The characters do not share the ironic view of the world implied in the adjective "prodigiosa." A more interesting and constant source of complicity involves what this critic has identified as the verbal formula "A pero B" ("A but B"). That is "X thought or believed A, *pero* ("but") it is really B." For example, the narrator states that Balthazar has "una expresión general de muchacho asustado. Pero era una expresión falsa" ("the general expression of a frightened boy. But it was a false expression," 106). García Márquez uses this formula regularly throughout this story. It is a way of placing the reader in a position consistently superior to the characters: they think A, *pero* (*"but"*) the reader (in complicity with the narrator) knows better.

"Balthazar's Marvelous Afternoon" is a statement about society and the artist's role in it. Three social classes are represented: the aristocracy by José Montiel, the middle class by Dr. Giraldo, and the lower-class artisan by Balthazar. Only the doctor places a monetary value on the cage. He examines the cage carefully and makes his calculated offer. The aristocrat José Montiel refuses to place a value on the cage, despite his obvious financial ability to purchase it if he wishes. His sense for financial matters is ridiculed with the narrator's observation that Montiel, as has been noted, had never smelled an odor that could not be sold. This revealing phrase is followed by a comma and the fact that he remains totally indifferent to the news of the cage. The ideologeme of the cage reveals a surprising anomaly: what the aristocrat (Montiel) and the marginal artist (Balthazar) have in common is their refusal to place monetary value on an object, something which only the middle class (Giraldo) is willing to do. Balthazar's key moment in this sense is not just his act of creation or celebration at the bar, but rather his giving the cage to Montiel's son. This act and the consequent parallel positions adopted by Montiel and Balthazar form a reenactment of the lines of dependence of earlier Western European societies in which the aristocrat and the artist were closely linked, but in which the artisan's work and virtue only serve to destroy him and to enrich the master. It is another example of not only a hierarchical society, but also an ineffective middle class.

The third of this trio of stories which share different aspects of humor is "The Day After Saturday." This, an early story of the volume, was awarded a prize in 1955 by the Association of Colombian Artists and Writers. García Márquez uses a technique that will be successfully exploited in his later fiction, such as *In Evil Hour* and "A Very Old Man with Enormous Wings": the entrance of an element foreign to society which interrupts its regular sense of order. The strange element is a growing number of dead birds that seem to be falling into all parts of the town. This odd situation occasions the breakdown of everyday order which provides García Márquez with his point of departure.

The problem is first brought to the reader's attention through Señora Rebecca, a widow who discovers that her house has been entered by someone unknown to her. She finds assurance when she goes to the mayor to report the problem: the first thing she sees is a pile of dead birds on his desk. She reports the problem of her house and suggests that local boys have been up to mischief. The mayor responds dryly that the problem is not the boys, but birds breaking into homes to die inside.

The entire town is concerned about the strange turn of events. They hardly notice the hot July weather in Macondo. Only a minority is willing to turn to the town's weak priest, the ninety-four-year-old Antonio Isabel Santísimo Sacramento del Altar Castañeda y Montero. He lost all credibility among the townfolk since the day he claimed to have seen the devil three times. At first the priest pays little attention to a few moribund animals. Once he encounters the third bird, however, he comes to the vague realization that something important is happening in the town. At the beginning he decides that the events do not merit a sermon.

One Saturday a bird falls at the priest's feet, right in front of Señora Rebecca's home. He decides it can still be saved. He and Señora Rebecca attempt to care for it. The bird dies, however, an event which leads the priest to question the situation more seriously, and finally realize that he had not even thought of one of the most obvious possibilities: the coming of the apocalypse. Nevertheless, he feels vaguely uncomfortable with both his explanation and the situation in general. As different memories are evoked in his mind by this strange series of events, he is afraid. Suddenly, he has a second revelation: the strange events are somehow related to the biblical story of the Wandering Jew.

At this point in the story, when some order seems near, García Márquez introduces yet another ambiguous element: a stranger who arrives by train. This boy gets off the train for lunch and misses its departure. The provincial boy, who had never seen electricity before, plans to leave the next day. He decides to see the aging and legendary priest give a sermon. The priest notices him in the congregation, his hat still on his head. The priest insists on the Wandering Jew interpretation to the end: he asks for a donation from the congregation to disinter the Wandering Jew. The story ends with the priest telling the altar boy to give this money to the stranger in the congregation, so he can purchase a new hat.

Two technical devices contribute to the success of this story. The first is the use of an inexplicable, irrational element which interrupts the regular order. Nevertheless, the characters will search for a logical explanation for this inexplicable phenomenon. The results can often be quite humorous. The second technical device is the use of a changing narrative focus. The narration remains a consistent third-person omniscient, but the narrator changes the focus from one character to another with no preparatory explanation for the reader. The combination of the unexplicable foreign element and the constantly changing narrative focus makes the experience of the story one of ambiguity, and experience which is not resolved but reinforced by the story's ending.

"One Day After Saturday" is an interesting commentary on authority. The two supposedly maximum figures of authority in the town, the mayor and the priest, are ideologemes for a decadent and impotent society. The reader can make this observation on the basis of their actions. In addition, García Márquez clearly defines their presence in the novel as authority figures: when Señora Rebecca discovers the problem, she is described as a person who goes to the mayor because she has a sense for "authority" (87). When she sees the dead birds in his office, the scene is described by the narrator as one of "autoridad degradada" (88) ("authority degraded," 123). The priest attempts to respond to the strange series of events as a way of maintaining a semblance of an authority figure.

The social and political implications of "One Day After Saturday" are evident. Two stories in this volume treat these matters directly in the Colombian context, dealing with the period of *la violencia.* These two stories as "One of These Days" and "Montiel's Widow." The former is one of the finest examples of García Márquez's ability to write devastatingly political fiction with his primary tool being understatement. The story's brevity is one indicator of this fact. It is a four-page anecdote that captures the subtleties of political conflict in a small town. The central character is a humble dentist who finds himself coerced by the mayor to treat the latter's toothache. The dentist's every move and word are an exercise in understatement. At the beginning of the story the dentist's son announces to him that the mayor has come for treatment; the dentist responds curtly "Tell him I'm not here" (73). After the threat of violence if he does not attend to the mayor, the dentist allows him to enter. The dentist responds to him with one-word phrases:

> —Siéntese.
> —Buenos días—dijo el alcalde.

—Buenos—dijo el dentista.

"Sit down."
"Good morning," said the Mayor.
"Morning," said the dentist. (24)

The frigidity of this interchange, which is notable in a language and culture which emphasizes lengthy salutory exchanges, marks the underlying tension between the two throughout the remainder of the story. When the dentist prepares his treatment of the abscessed tooth, he says and does everything without ever looking the mayor in the eye. The one direct communication, which makes the story explicitly political, is the one-sentence statement the dentist makes at the outset of his operation: "Aquí nos paga veinte muertos, teniente" (25) ("Now you'll pay for our twenty dead men," 75). The dentist then operates, without anesthesia. The perspective moves to the mayor; rather than describing the cruel process itself, García Márquez tells of the pain the mayor feels and the tears that come from his eyes.

The dentist's revenge, a reaction of a bourgeois professional on behalf of the humble masses before the powerful mayor, is only a token, very momentary act. This fact is clear with the story's final lines, when the dentist asks if he should send the bill directly to the mayor or the municipal government. When the mayor responds "Es la misma vaina" ("It's the same damn thing," 76), it is an indicator that the institutional power structure, despite these moments of the mayor's vulnerability, remains intact: the mayor can still do whatever he wishes in the name of the government.

A different facet of the power structure and its relationship to *la violencia* is explored in "Montiel's Widow." In "One of These Days" there is a clear awareness on the part of the dominated (the humble dentist) of the class structure. It is a story about the confrontation of the powerful and the powerless. "'Montiel's Widow" deals with the oligarchy and those who are unaware of its functioning. José Montiel is the oligarch par excellence. He has already died at the story's outset; his wife is the character innocent of her husband's actions.

José Montiel's actions can be read as a complete list of the possibilities of local political chicanery: political murders, monopolizing of local businesses by terror, and well-conceived massacres. The most notable feature of his domination is not the exploitation of the poor, but the elimination of potential competition among the local oligarchy. Having eliminated all opposition, he establishes himself as the most rich and powerful person in the town. The presence of his wife in the story makes it more incredible than even exceptional political maneuvering: she is never conscious of the situation. To the contrary, she pities the dead that she has no idea are the result of her own husband's actions. The pious widow prays for them. She can be read as an ideologeme for that sector of society that supports its institutions, and even institutionalized violence, without realizing the true nature of either.

Three stories which cannot easily be categorized within the confines of those discussed above are "Tuesday Siesta," "There Are No Thieves in This Town," and "Artificial Roses." They are, above all, stories about people and their special qualities, and human situations. García Márquez portrays the plight of the poor. Rather than attempting to gain the reader's sympathy for these people by underlining their misery, he exalts their qualities.

"Tuesday Siesta" deals with just such a characterization, dealing with a poor woman who arrives in a small town in a third-class car of a train, looking for the place where her son has been buried. Her twelve-year-old daughter accompanies her. The town is resting during siesta upon their arrival. The first exchange of words in the town, between her and the woman caring for the priest's home, indicates her stark urgency:

> —Necesito al padre—dijo.
> —Ahora está durmiendo.
> —Es urgente—insistió la mujer. (14)

> "I need the priest," she said.
> "He's sleeping now."
> "It's an emergency," the woman insisted. (68)

She is a woman of few words who speaks with a convincing directness. Her conversation with the priest reveals that her son was killed the previous week during an attempted robbery. During this conversation, she maintains the same smooth posture noted in the brief dialogue with the woman: "A medida que llenaba la hoja pedía a la mujer los datos de su identidad, y ella respondía sin vacilación, con detalles precisos, como si estuviera leyendo" (16) ("As he filled the page, he asked the woman to identify herself, and she replied unhesitatingly, with precise details, as if she were reading them," (69). Her most important line until the end of the story is her response to the priest's inquiries about her son's character: "Yo le decía que nunca robara nada que le hiciera falta a alguien para comer, y él me hacía caso" (18) ("I told him never to steal anything that anyone needed to eat, and he minded me," 71).

At the end of the story, the priest and his sister attempt to save the couple from the potential embarrassment of walking through the town, suffering its opprobrium. The priest suggests they wait until the sun goes down. His sister offers to lend them a parasol, ostensibly for the sun, but it is understood that it will protect them from severe stares. The mother refuses curtly: "Gracias—replicó la mujer. Así vamos bien." (19) ("Thank you," replied the woman. "We're all right this way," 72). She takes her daughter by her hand and goes out into the street.

"Tuesday Siesta" is a story about human dignity. Despite her social class and her family's reputation in the town, the mother firmly maintains her self-esteem. At the story's end the reader does not just sympathize with this poor woman, but admires her. Dignity and respect are also important in "There Are No Thieves in This Town," although they are not portrayed as poignantly. "There Are No Thieves in This Town" also has the suspense of a mystery, an example of García Márquez's continued interest in just telling a good story. The plot involves a robbery committed by the central character, Dámaso. The importance of this "robbery" seems grossly exaggerated in this small town: Dámaso steals three billiard balls from a tavern. He takes them because there was not any money or other goods. The tavern owner claims two hundred pesos (a few dollars) have been stolen too.

Dámaso's wife reacts in the same way as the reader she wonders why he would even bother to steal the billiard balls. In the town, however, the theft is the event of the year. It becomes the talk of the town, subject to the numerous and contradictory versions of what has happened. In such a small, honest, and even innocent town, the effect of three missing billiard balls is like a death. Moreover, the missing game objects interrupt the entire order of the town. The virtually irreplaceable balls are a central part of the town's social life. The plot offers two possible results of the crime. Everyone is convinced of his guilt. On the other hand, Dámaso's successful pilfering leads to fantasies of more absurd adventures of this sort: he speaks with his wife of stealing balls in one town and selling them in another. Eventually the pressure of the situation, however, leads the couple to search for a solution to the problem, a way of ridding themselves of the balls. His wife does not like the idea of simply abandoning the balls in a public place, because such a solution would not solve the black man's predicament. The tension created by the situation results in a deteriorization of the husband-wife relationship and physical violence. In the end, Dámaso is apprehended returning the balls, and it is evident that he will be made to suffer for his theft.

This is not one of the most subtle or refined stories of the volume. The mystery element is more important than the portrayal of character. It should be seen primarily as an exercise in storytelling, like many of the stories published before 1955. It shows some of the stylistic characteristics of Hemingway, from whom García Márquez was learning. [15] Within the context provided by Ong, for example, it could be pointed out that García Márquez uses "esa" ("that") in a way similar to Hemingway to gain the approval of the reader: "y sus movimientos tenían *esa* suave eficacia de la gente acostumbrada a la realidad" (32; my italics) ("and her movements had the gentle efficiency of people who are used to reality," 80). The "esa" of the original Spanish (lost in the translation) refers to an efficiency that both the writer and reader know about, a knowledge they previously share.

The humble being whose dignity García Márquez portrays in "Artificial Roses" is a young woman named Mina. She seems to be trapped between a difficult grandmother and her own limited economic situation. She misses mass because she is not able to find her total attire, having lost her sleeves. She knows she will not be able to receive communion with her shoulders uncovered. Her predicament at home is even worse: she must make one hundred and fifty dozen artificial roses by Easter. The story neither elaborates on her situation in great detail nor leads to a powerful conclusion: the overworked Mina maintains her dignity in the end by confronting her grandmother's excessively personal inquiries about the details of her personal life.

The stories of *Big Mama's Funeral* represent the uniformly successful result of a young professional writer in search of a sophisticated form of expression of social and political realities. They also introduce the element of humor that showed initial traces in *Leafstorm*. The type of humor ranges from the raucous hyperbole of "Big Mama's Funeral" to the understatement of other stories. The exuberant heteroglossia of "Big Mama's Funeral," on the other hand, is reduced to the minimal sterility of language in stories such as "Tuesday Siesta" or "One of These Days." A traditional, hierarchical and often corrupt society is fictionalized through the use of a variety of ideologemes. The correspondence between narrative point of view and ideology can be appreciated in these stories by observing the human filters García Márquez uses to relate these stories: humble persons who maintain their dignity despite the power of the hierarchy above them. They are often reduced to silence, an appropriation of the word that cannot steal from them their profound humanity. A type of discourse of silence is the most outstanding characteristic of the next book, *No One Writes to the Colonel*.

No One Writes to the Colonel (1961)

The silence of *No One Writes to the Colonel* is inscribed by an articulated and also a nonarticulated political censorship. The book's protagonist, an aged colonel, as well as Macondo's other inhabitants, avoid political language at all costs. The political situation is the essential and overriding factor in everyone's life. Consequently, the existence of this minimalized political discourse, resulting in a discourse of silence, is the novel's outstanding feature.

The work's structure and plot are one level of reduction of the fiction to its barest essentials. It is a short novel (92 pages in the Spanish edition) which tells the story of the colonel and life in a small town in a simple, straightforward style. The fact that the novel's "present" is the mid-1950s is quite important because it is a period of intense political violence and repression in Colombia. The seventy-five-year-old protagonist was a colonel in the War of a Thousand Days (1899–1902) at the age of twenty. He fought along side Colonel Buendía, a well-known figure from García Márquez's other books. At the end of the war the protagonist came to the coastal town of Neerlandia, where the treaty was signed. A faction of the rebels who arose against the establishment consisted of Colonel Auerliano Buendía and the duke of Marlborough. The colonel had arrived in Neerlandia precisely to turn over funds for this revolutionary cause to Colonel Buendía. After the war he lived in Macondo. Like the characters in *Leafstorm,* however, he suffers from the decadence brought by the banana fever during the early part of the twentieth century. Consequently, he leaves Macondo in 1906. He marries during the midteens and his son, Agustín, is born in 1922. He spends the rest of his life awaiting the check for the military pension, a letter which never arrives.

The action takes place during a period of about three months, from October to December. From the very beginning of the novel it is clear that the colonel lives a poor life: he struggles to even make some coffee from the little that he has left in his dirty pot. It soon becomes known that his son Agustín was shot nine months before for circulating clandestine political literature. Agustín leaves the colonel a fighting cock which the latter plans to use as his last resort, his financial saviour. The animal offers several types of symbolic readings. On the one hand, it represents hope, something very important for the colonel in the novel. Angel Rama has pointed out that the association between the cock's struggle and the youth dedicated to political struggle is inevitable.[16] Vargas Llosa, in response to Rama, maintains that the cock does not symbolize the same thing for everyone.[17] For the colonel's wife, it is a sign of craziness. On the other hand, it has only commercial value for Don Sabas.

The basic setting and situations of this novel present a dismal picture of violence and depravity. Like some of the short stories from this period, however, *No One Writes to the Colonel* also contains humor. The situations do not generally lend themselves easily to humor, although the colonel's predicament does offer some element of humor just on the basis of its fundamental absurdity. The main source of humor, as in "Big Mama's Funeral," is language itself. The characters often say funny things, especially the colonel. Near the beginning of the novel, a group of boys gathers around to watch the cock, so the colonel tells them: "No miren más a ese animal. Los gallos se gastan de tanto mirarlos"[18] ("Stop looking at that animal. Roosters wear out if you look at them so much," 5). Later, he discusses airplanes that are capable of flying above storms. The colonel ends the conversation with the comment "Por supuesto. Debe ser como las alfombras" (33). ("Naturally. It must be like a carpet," 21). The humor is created in each of these quotes, and others, because the colonel's comments are totally out of the normal context for such a situation.

The constant but subtle references to the political situation make the book above all one about politics. Both generations of the novel's family have been rendered neutral, impotent, by established authority: the ex-revolutionary colonel waits hopelessly for nonexistent financial support; the son has been assassinated because of his supposedly subversive political activity. There are blatant facts of daily life in this town, but facts which absolutely no one discusses. On the one hand, political discourse is controlled by government censorship. When the colonel asks the doctor about news in the newspapers, the doctor responds: "Es difícil leer entre líneas lo que permite publicar la censura" (21) ("It's hard to read between the lines which the censor lets them print," 13). The old language of the church controls the new language of modernity—modern films— by means of censorship too: the sound of church bells indicates whether or not films have church approval. Other facts indicate that the political situation is threatening: even a funeral procession cannot pass through town because it is in "estado de sitio"—a state of siege.[19] All members of a political party were eliminated in this town too, with the exception of Don Sabas.

Political repression has reduced the richness of potential heteroglossia to a barren discourse of silence. As in "Tuesday Siesta" and "One of These Days," language in this novel tends toward uniform sterility. As the colonel says with respect to the government: "Pero hace como cinco años que no dicen nada" (22) ("But it's been about five years since they've said anything," 14). It is a novel in which amazingly little is ever said. At one point the doctor gives the colonel a clandestine newspaper, saying, interestingly enough, "Es lo que no decían los periódicos de ayer" (25). ("That's what the newspapers didn't print yesterday," 16). Even the clandestine newspaper is a reduction by its very nature: its mimeographed format necessarily limits its possibilities of production and its underground distribution necessarily limits its number of readers. The most outstanding ideologeme for this discourse of silence is a sign hanging in the tailor's shop: "Prohibido hablar de política" (51) ("Talking Politics Forbidden," 33).

Despite the dismal political situation, and the portrayal of a people reduced to silence, the total vision presented in the novel is not entirely negative. The firm dignity of certain characters in the stories is recalled in the more fragile—but constant—dignity of the colonel. He never gives up faith that his heroic acts in war will be justly compensated. There is a general sense in the novel that, if one does not give up faith, both the individual and the collective destinies can be improved. One critic has described this general sense, appropriately enough, as a fundamental optimism.[20] This is an early example of the basic affirmation for humanity found in García Márquez's later work, most notably the masterpiece that will later synthesize all this fiction of Macondo, *One Hundred Years of Solitude.* One more step in the apprenticeship and total creation of Macondo will be necessary before the writing of this masterpiece, this last short novel being *In Evil Hour.*

In Evil Hour (1962)

No One Writes to the Colonel is a subtle novel that communicates the implications of political repression of the period of *la violencia* in Colombia. *In Evil Hour* deals with the same basic situation, but the presentation is much more direct; violence and other physical acts are visible. Subversion and repression are not the nonarticulated taboo subjects of clandestine newspapers or conversations, but the central actions of the novel, which tells the story of life in an unnamed town during seventeen days, from the fourth of October to the twenty-first.

The reader acquainted with García Márquez's earlier books discussed in this chapter will note that *In Evil Hour* involves a certain synthesizing process that will be intensified later in *One Hundred Years of Solitude:* several characters and situations from the previous stories appear in *In Evil Hour.* The recognizable characters include Don Sabas, Father Angel, and the mayor from *No One Writes to the Colonel.* Another sign will be displayed that prohibits talk about politics. The dentist from "One of These Days" appears again, once more inflicting pain on the mayor. In addition, the reader encounters the Montiel family from "Balthazar's Marvelous Afternoon" and "Montiel's Widow," Mina and Trinidad from "Artificial Roses," and Don Roque from "In This Town There Are No Thieves," among other characters.

In Evil Hour consists of ten unnumbered chapters, a total of forty brief sections, which present a panoramic view of life in the town. The use of these sections and montage techniques make the novel an experience for the reader of organizing a story, rather than following a linear story line, as is offered in *No One Writes to the Colonel.*

A certain story, with subplots, does emerge. The first chapter, which contains four brief three- to four-page sections, deals with a character named César Montero. The first section of this chapter focuses on Father Angel, preoccupied with daily life in the church in his conversation with Trinidad, his helper. Two seemingly insignificant details of this section will become important in the remainder of this chapter and the novel. First, Father Angel and Trinidad briefly comment on the clarinet music which they hear Pastor playing in the background. Next, at the very end of the chapter, Trinidad mentions that he has seen "pasquines"—lampoons that have been appearing recently on the walls of the town. They accuse members of the local oligarchy of scandalous activities. In the next section César Montero reads one of the pieces of paper stuck on the wall of his home. He rips up the lampoon, and then proceeds directly to methodically shoot Pastor. The next section switches the focus to the mayor, who has to handle this scandal. He orders Pastor's body to be taken for an autopsy. The fourth and final section of this chapter focuses on Father Angel, as the first. His reaction to the death is to prohibit the showing of a film in the local movie house that night. No such entertainment should be permitted during the mourning.

The remaining nine chapters are structured in a fashion similar to the first. The focus changes in the different sections, and the reader provides the links between them. The second chapter deals with the death and the lampoons introduced in the first, but the central focus here, as in the remainder of the novel, is the lampoons. Town authorities, such as Judge Arcadio, discuss the possible origin of the scandalous public notes. Roberto Assis, one of the town's distinguished citizens, is the victim of a lampoon accusing his wife of infidelity. The third chapter provides a broader picture of the political situation in the town and nation, characterized by its precarious stability maintained by repression. Here the two political anecdotes from previous stories appear: the sign prohibiting talk of politics and the dentist getting revenge on the mayor by means of an excruciatingly painful tooth abstraction. The dentist refuses to use anesthesia and makes it clear that political revenge is the motive for his making the mayor suffer so much. Chapters 4 through 7 continue along the same lines, with increasing concern over the lampoons and focus on the same small group of town authorities.

A radical change in the development of the story takes place in chapter 8. The threat of subversion offered by the lampoons is realized with the appearance of a clandestine newspaper. More importantly, it results in overt repression of the sort that had characterized life in the town in the past: the mayor abolishes civil liberties and encarcerates Pepe Amador, the distributor of the clandestine newspaper. As one of the town's citizens observes in this chapter, things are just as they were before. In the last two chapters the repression increases and the potential subversion and reaction to it on the part of the town's authorities results in a situation of war. Dissidents have departed to the mountains to join guerrillas; the mayor himself admits that the area is in a state of war.

The catalyst of these actions and events is, once again, an element foreign to established reality which interrupts the regular order of things. In the stories of *Big Mama's Funeral,* García Márquez had used elements such as pigeons, the absence of billiard balls, and death to then create a fiction around the results of the breakdown of order. The lampoons serve this mechanical function in this story. Unlike pigeons and the billiard balls, however, the lampoons are more than simply mechanical devices. One critic has proposed that they symbolize resistance to the order imposed upon the town.[21] This is undoubtedly true; in addition, they are an ideologeme. They are a metaphor for literature itself as a form of resistance or protest.[22] Several obvious indicators in the text justify such a reading. One is the fact that the lampoons, like literature, are a written and public form of communication. The writer of novels, unable to display his texts in public beyond bookstore windows, often uses posters to decorate walls just as these lampoons do in this town. In a conversation between Doctor Giraldo and Don Sabas, the latter actually describes the lampoons as novels:

—Mucho cuidado, doctor, que no me quiero morir sin saber cómo termina esta novela.
—¿Cuál novela?
—Los pasquines.[23]

"Be very careful, Doctor. I don't want to die without finding out how this novel comes out."
"What novel?"
"The lampoons."[24]

Shortly thereafter, in another conversation, the judge claims that this matter of the lampoons "Es como leer novelas policíacas" (117) ("It's like reading detective stories," 104). These quotations make explicit the connection between the lampoons and literature. They share implicit characteristics too. The lampoons, like literature, are a form of subversion that is, at the most, a catalyst: they are not capable of effecting social change or revolution in themselves, but they can create a level of awareness that may result in action later. The lampoons seem to lead to the clandestine newspaper, just as written literature can lead to a protest march or the formation of political parties.

It has been proposed that all fiction finds its origins in rumor, gossip. True or not as a generalization, rumor is certainly an important factor in much Spanish-American fiction and the work of García Márquez. The common roots in rumor are one more characteristic that these lampoons and literature share. Several characters in the novel observe that the lampoons say nothing that is not already rumored in the town. The widow Montiel says something to Doctor Giraldo in this respect which is quite appropriate. She equates rumor with the creation of lampoons: "Por Dios, doctor, no sea tan chismoso. Usted debe ser el que pone los pasquines" (156) ("Good heavens, Doctor, don't be so gossipy. You must be the one who's putting up the lampoons," 140). It would have been only a minor substitution, of little notice for the doctor or most readers, if she had said "You must be the one who writes novels." In a way, then, this is a novel about fiction. More important, it is a novel about the nature of subversion and disorder in society, and thus a defense of literature as a legitimate contribution to revolutionary process.

No One Writes to the Colonel was the subtle novel of silence; like the town's readers of official newspapers, it required reading between the lines and even interpretation of what was not stated. It communicates the intangible consequences of silence, such as the quiet dignity underlying the colonel's behavior. *In Evil Hour* is a novel of what is said; it demonstrates the tangible consequences of the articulated (spoken and written) word. As has been pointed out, the lampoons print what is already being said among the townspeople. Or as one character states: "Pero sólo dicen lo que ya anda diciendo la gente" (37) ("But they only tell what people are already saying," 30). Not only is it established knowledge, but it seems to be basically well-founded information. As the doctor says about the lampoons "Dicen lo que todo el mundo sabe, que por cierto es casi siempre la verdad" (102) ("They say what everybody knows, which is almost always sure to be the truth," 90). Given the level of repression that exists in the town and, knowing its recent history, the even higher level of potential repression, the articulation of social and political realities is not totally open and free. The lampoons exist, as does political conversation, but only because the authorities cannot control them. Mr. Carmichael states, feeling the need to speak more than the situation seems to allow: "Es que uno está que se revienta por hablar" (53) ("It's just that a person is busting with talk," 44).

The narrator also provides a much more explicit and visible exposition of the characters, a type of presentation and background lacking in *No One Writes to the Colonel*. For example, in the earlier novel it is understood that the priest is somehow censoring the town's films with his church bells, but the narrator offered no details. In this novel the narrator provides the reader with Father Angel's thoughts, motives, and procedures. In *No One Writes to the Colonel*, the reader knows that Don Sabas has somehow managed to be the only member of the opposition party allowed to remain in the town, but it is never known precisely what kind of political deal he made to satisfy those now in power. Near the end of *In Evil Hour* a conversation between Carmichael and the mayor reveals that Don Sabas had given José Montiel a complete list of the people in contact with the guerrillas in exchange for the right to remain in the town.

In Evil Hour is a successful and satisfying reading experience, but not for the same reasons as the previous stories and the short novel; narrative technique has changed. García Márquez's handling of the murder of Pastor in the first chapter is a superb example of his basic narrative procedure. The third-person omniscient narrator who narrates all the scenes relates the anecdote in a distant fashion. He does not explain Montero's thoughts or feelings. Rather, the reader follows his actions, from the discovery of the lampoon to the pulling of the trigger of his gun. Then, just as important, there is virtually no description of the actual death of Pastor. The essential matter here is not moving the reader with the emotion of a death, but showing the variety of reactions to it by different members of the town: the next three scenes describe these reactions in three different places immediately following the death. Rather than a detailed bloody scene, the reader experiences an impersonal procedure of exterior reality.[25] This type of description is the standard procedure used throughout the novel.

This novel's most successful technical innovation, considered in the total trajectory of García Márquez's work, is the use of montage. By juxtaposing different scenes that take place at approximately the same time, he creates a sense of simultaneity. In addition, the reader is privy to a wide variety of situations in the town, getting a panoramic view. The transitions from one scene to another, for example, in the first chapter indicate how the montage effect functions. The first scene involves a conversation between Father Angel and Trinidad. The scene ends with the conversation simply being cut off. Then, as if the reader were perceiving the town through a moving camera lens, the scene moves in the second section of the chapter, as follows: "Tres casas más allá, César Montero soñaba con los elefantes" (10) ("Three houses beyond, César Montero was dreaming about elephants," 4). The use of the term "más allá" relates the section to the first one, and creates the sense of simultaneity: the reader realizes that he/she will find out what Montero is doing while this conversation is taking place between Father Angel and Trinidad. At the end of the section, Montero kills Pastor; he pulls the trigger in the last paragraph. The first line in the third section is as follows: "El alcalde empezaba a dormirse en el momento del disparo" (14) ("The mayor had begun to fall asleep at the moment of the shot," 8). This sentence thus links the mayor's scene to the previous one in time. These three scenes are the ones in this chapter which fit together most closely in time. Unlike García Márquez's very first stories, in which play with reality was an end in itself, here the writer uses his technical ability to provide a broader sense of reality: each of these three scenes, in a certain way, is a "behind the scene" special reality when juxtaposed with one another.

Attention has been paid throughout this study to those key points in García Márquez's work in which a conglomerate of different languages is employed. As has been pointed out, Bakhtin has created the term "heteroglossia" for this presence of a variety of languages in a text.[26] The extent to which heteroglossia is traceable and important in García Márquez's writing varies from text to text. The case of *In Evil Hour* merits a brief incursion into the background of Bakhtin's proposition about language. Being an early twentieth-century Russian theorist, Bakhtin used nineteenth-century Russia as his most immediate literary frame of reference. He noted the correspondence between the decadence of society and the flourishing of languages—heteroglossia—in novels. The heteroglossia observable in Latin American writers such as García Márquez represents more than just a technical characteristic. It is also a residue of a society both in flux and in a process of decay in some ways comparable to societies such as nineteenth-century Russia. One of Latin America's most authoritative writers and critics, Mario Vargas Llosa, has proposed, coincidentally, that it is precisely societies in decay that produce the most vital literature. This is one of the reasons, according to Vargas Llosa, for Latin America's present position at the forefront of world literature.

Returning specifically to *In Evil Hour* the reader can note first that it was written in a society in crisis and about a society in decadence. The order maintained by the trio most present in the novel—the mayor, the judge, and the priest—is only a superficial harmony, the sugar coating on a decaying organism. Its fragility is evidenced by the fact that some public notes can threaten its existence so much. As Mr. Benjamin states appropriately in a conversation with the dentist, concerning the lampoons, "Es un síntoma de descomposición social" (122) ("It's a symptom of social decomposition," 108). A comparison of the mayor's handling of the two deaths demonstrates how true Benjamin's statement is. When Pastor was murdered, the mayor followed institutional formalities by ordering an autopsy. Once the fragile order of the town has been placed into doubt by lampoons and a clandestine newspaper, and the superficial appearance of health unearthed to reveal society's fundamental decadence, the mayor conscientiously ignores formalities and orders that no autopsy be performed on Pepe Amador.

The conflicts between individuals and groups are also articulated by both the narrator and characters as conflicts of language in a novel rich in heteroglossia. Various types of institutional language are in constant opposition to the language of change. The rumors and gossip which are probably the most accurate indicators of the town's moral and social fabric are not threatening to the town's authorities because such language occupies no space in the institutional framework. It does not have permanence either; it can be forgotten or modified and quite often is. The lampoons occupy an ambiguous space between this gossip and institutional language. Like gossip this language seems to spring from the common knowledge of all the townfolk; being written it has the threatening potential of public recognition and permanence. The lampoons are not political in content, so they are threatening to the official institutional language only in the sense that they can potentially destroy the social cohesion and unity of the town. The language of the clandestine newspaper, however, is in direct opposition to the institutional language of the mayor, the judge, and the priest, the novel's three representatives of the power structure.

With the exception of the lampoons and the clandestine newspaper at the end, the heteroglossia of *In Evil Hour* is limited to institutional language. As the barber says, "Ya no quedan en el país sino los periódicos oficiales . . ." (51) ("The only newspapers left in the country are the official ones . . . ," 43). The narrator uses the language of the church to describe the ailing mayor, suffering from a toothache: "Rezó a fondo, tensos los músculos en el espasmo final, pero consciente de que mientras más pugnaba por lograr el contacto con Dios, con más fuerza lo empujaba el dolor en sentido contrario" (65) ("He prayed deeply, his muscles tense in the final spasm, but aware that the more he struggled to make contact with God, the greater the force of the pain to push him in the opposite direction," 54). His own official language is perhaps best exemplified with one short statement he makes to Moises: "El pueblo progresa" (79) ("The town's making progress," 69). Here he captures the essence of what his institutional program is supposedly effecting: a democratic and progressive government. César Montero, in a conversation with the mayor, uses the mayor's language of democracy and progress to question its effectiveness: "Ahora el nuevo gobierno ha decidido que haya paz y garantías para todos y yo sigo reventando con mi sueldo mientras tú te pudres en plata" (85) ("Now the new government has decided that there should be peace and guarantees for everybody and I go on being broke on my salary while you're filthy with money," 74). At the end of the novel the social decomposition has led to a situation of a civil war which will be fought during a period after the novel's close. Institutional language, however, prevails to the end: the mayor declares that there will be no autopsy (for Pepe Amador) because "no hay muerto"—there has been no death. Language that can control life and death, of course, is the language of power.

No One Writes to the Colonel and *In Evil Hour* deal with the same period in Colombia's history and touch upon similar themes. Difference in structure and technique, nevertheless, make them radically different. The reader in *No One Writes to the Colonel* participates in a game of complicity with the narrator, sharing with him in the nonarticulated but understood situation in the town. Unlike the doggedly optimistic colonel, the reader and the narrator realize that no letter will come. The novel's optimism originates not in the real possibility of a change on the part of the ruling establishment, but in the fortitude of one individual, the colonel. The reader in *In Evil Hour* is not able to adopt such a superior role. Like the inhabitants in the town, the reader must use the clues available to them in order to attempt to make sense of the lampoons and discover their creator. As one character says, experiencing the same as the reader, it is like reading a detective novel. García Márquez has found yet another way to actively involve his reader in the process of fiction. The most experiential of all his novels will be the next and culminating stage in his writing career, the magnificent *One Hundred Years of Solitude*.

Chapter Four
One Hundred Years
of Solitude (1967)

One Hundred Years of Solitude is an utter joy to read yet, paradoxically, an elusive book to write about. What we most enjoy reading is not necessarily the same as what we can most comfortably explain or analyze. Nevertheless, observations, commentaries, and studies on specific aspects of this novel abound. The very fact that it is already one of the most written-about novels in all of Latin American literature indicates something about the experience of reading it. For beginning students of literature, first discovering literary texts as a symbolic form of communication, this is a novel replete with the symbols that are often the focus of discussion in literature classes. For the casual reader of popular fiction, it has the story line and action of the best-seller. Literary critics of virtually any persuasion—myth critics, archetype specialists, structuralists, or whatever—find in this novel a gold mine of material to support their theories or upon which to construct their readings. The panoply of different and even contradictory readings has led García Márquez to comment that critics, unlike novelists, find "not what they can, but what they want."[1]

Most readers and critics would probably agree that a single reading of almost any novel is usually incomplete. In the case of this overwhelmingly and exasperatingly rich novel, however, most readings seem grossly inadequate, falling short of communicating the total experience of the novel. It has often been called a "total novel," a term popularized in the Spanish-speaking world by Mario Vargas Llosa. Once one understands and accepts the implications and limits of attempting to discuss such a "total" novel in an introductory fashion, some commentary is possible. The present chapter is divided into four parts: (1) an introduction with a resumé of the plot, (2) an overview of the principal trends of thought among critics and readers of the novel, (3) the social and political implications, and (4) narrative technique and the universality of this novel.

Introduction and Plot

One Hundred Years of Solitude is the story of the Buendía family
and the story of Macondo. José Arcadio Buendía marries his cousin,
Ursula, and they are the illustrious first generation of a prodigious
seven-generation family. Because of their kinship, José Arcadio
Buendía and Ursula, and like them, all of their descendants, live
upon the threat and terror of engendering a child with a pig's tail.
The novel can also be described as the story of Macondo, which is
founded by José Arcadio Buendía. Macondo progresses from a primitive village to a modern town, after the arrival of electricity, lights,
and other twentieth-century conveniences. It also suffers the vicis-
situdes of Colombia's history, including its civil wars.

The story of the Buendías in Macondo is very entertaining. Of
García Márquez's books, *One Hundred Years of Solitude* is the novel
which has had by far the most appeal and widest acceptance by the
international reading public. John S. Brushwood has suggested that
this broad appeal is based on three factors.[2] First, García Márquez
insists on the right to invent his own reality. He allows a free reign
to imagination, resulting in a remarkably inventive fiction. For
example, it is one in which a character might fly off on a carpet or
the entire town might forget the names of even the most everyday
objects. Second, the novel has not just one, but several interest-
provoking characteristics: unusual people, fantasy, and plot suspense
are among the most notable. The unusual people who populate or
visit Macondo include almost everyone, from José Arcadio Buendía
to the last Buendía, with the tail, for everyone in this fictional world
either has or soon acquires exaggerated proportions. The third factor
is that it is a very funny novel. Like much humorous literature, it
is also quite serious. Some of the most hilarious passages, for example, are those which satirize institutions or types of persons typical
of Latin American society.

One Hundred Years of Solitude consists of twenty unnumbered and
untitled chapter-length sections. (For the sake of simplicity, they
will be identified as "chapters" in this discussion.) They tell the
story of the Buendía family and Macondo in a basically linear fashion,
with occasional diversions into the past or future. The first two
chapters provide the background to the family. The first focuses
primarily on José Arcadio Buendía's bizarre and even crazy methods
for attempting to understand the world. Amazed with the magnet

that the gypsy Melquíades has introduced to Macondo, José Arcadio declares that the real value for this useless invention is to extract gold from the earth. The next incredible inventions the gypsies bring, and of which he must try to make use, are a telescope and a magnifying glass. The practical-minded Ursula shows little patience with his scientific speculation. After days of intense study and contemplation, he declares to the family his latest discovery: "The earth is round, like an orange." At this point Ursula totally loses her patience, and informs him that if he is to go crazy, he will have to do so alone. The gypsies occasionally return with more modern inventions, but at the beginning little changes in this idyllic town of 300 citizens, where no one is over thirty years old and no one has yet died. It is a tropical paradise. Of the children, the older son, José Arcadio, is quiet and physically well-endowed. The younger Aureliano, the first person born in Macondo, seems to have supernatural powers, predicting that a pot would fall from a table, for example, seconds before it falls. The first chapter ends with Melquíades introducing José Arcadio Buendía to ice. After paying to touch it a second time, the patriarch declares that it is "the great invention of our time."

The second chapter moves back in the history of the family and describes the foundation of Macondo. It carries the family roots back to the sixteenth century, when Sir Francis Drake attacked the Colombian coastal region of Riohacha. Ursula's great-grandmother was wounded in the exchange of fire. Soon thereafter she and her husband moved inland, where her spouse established business relations with a tobacco farmer, Don José Arcadio Buendía. Several centuries later, Ursula's great-granddaughter, of the same name, would marry the great-grandson of Don José Arcadio Buendía, also, of course, of the same name. An uncle of José Arcadio Buendía had married an aunt of Ursula, resulting in the birth of a child with a pig's tail. Consequently, José Arcadio Buendía and Ursula spent months without consummating their marriage. Once his masculinity is ridiculed in public by his friend Prudencio Aguilar, however, José Arcadio Buendía gives his wife a complete demonstration of his *machismo,* resulting in the birth of their first son—without a pig's tail. He also kills Prudencio Aguilar, a death which haunts him and Ursula so much that they decide they must leave the town. They found a town which they name Macondo. Some of the family's history is less fantastic than the events described above: a daughter is born, Amaranta; the

son, José Arcadio, falls in love with Pilar Ternera. José Arcadio
Buendía continues to devote himself feverishly to his scientific experimentation. Ursula suddenly disappears, only to return unex-
pectedly five months later, having discovered a route to a nearby
town connected with the mail system and enjoying the amenities
of modern life.

The people Ursula brings to Macondo contribute to its transformation to a more modern town. In the third chapter more outsiders
arrive. The first is Rebecca, an orphan who arrives at the Buendía
home with a note from a distant relative of the family. She prefers
to eat dirt. Melquíades returns, bored with the solitude of death.
Macondo then suffers the intrusion of the government, which sends
a magistrate, Don Apolinar Moscote. He has two daughters, Amparo
and Remedios, the latter so beautiful that she will eventually be
referred to as "Remedios la bella." The son Aureliano feels pain
recalling even the image of Remedios's beauty. The new official is
not really accepted in the town, but a compromise is reached: he
will be allowed to stay, provided that he allows Macondo's citizens
to paint their homes the political color they wish and that the soldiers
who had accompanied him leave.[3]

One of the most curious episodes of chapter 3 is an insomnia
plague which afflicts Macondo. No one can sleep, despite the various
methods they invent to attempt to overcome the insomnia. With
it comes the lack of memory, a problem for which José Amparo
Buendía invents solutions. He places little signs on the most basic
everyday objects, carefully explaining their function. At the entrance
to the town he places a sign identifying the town: "Macondo." Next
to the sign, a larger one reminds the potentially forgetful: "God
exists." He even invents a "memory machine" with fourteen thousand entries. Melquíades finally gives the suffering population a
magic potion which cures them of their illness.

The new outsider who arrives in the fourth chapter is Pietro
Crespi, the artist. This handsome and elegant Italian comes to
Macondo to teach it the art of the pianola: his labors include as-
sembling the instrument, instructing purchasers in its function, and
giving music lessons. The ubiquitous Melquíades dies once again
in this chapter, for the second time. They give him a magnificent
funeral, described as the best since Big Mama's. (This mention
recalls the previous story of the same title.) Having taken care of
that deceased person, José Arcadio Buendía must deal with another

person who returns from death: Prudencio Aguilar. (His return also recalls the earlier fiction, as the narrator refers to a "death within death," a phrase from the 1948–52 period.) One of the outstanding anecdotes in this chapter is the growing love affair between Aureliano and Remedios. He becomes obsessed with her, writing poems about her incessantly, including on all the walls of the house. Finally, José Arcadio Buendía asks Apolinar Moscote for the hand of his daughter for his son.

The marriage between Aureliano and Remedios takes place at the beginning of the fifth chapter. The bride is still much an adolescent and in other ways just a young child. Apolinar Moscote, the magistrate, has functioned as nothing more than a token representative of the government up to this point. Much of the novel from chapter 5, however, concerns national, social, and political realities affecting Macondo. A considerable portion of this part of the novel is based on the real history of Colombia. For example, in the fifth chapter the two traditional parties in Colombia, the Liberals and the Conservatives, emerge for the first time. Aureliano receives an unambiguous lesson from his father-in-law about the Liberals:

Los liberales, le decía, eran masones; gente de mala índole, partidaria de ahorcar a los curas, de implantar el matrimonio civil y el divorcio, de reconocer iguales derechos a los hijos naturales que a los legítimos, y de despedazar al país en un sistema federal que despojara de poderes a la autoridad suprema.[4]

The Liberals, he said, were Freemasons, bad people, wanting to hang priests, to institute civil marriage and divorce, to recognize the rights of illegitimate children as equal to those of legitimate ones, and to cut the country up into a federal system that would take power away from the supreme authority.[5]

Such language is one indicator of the intensity of the division between Liberals and Conservatives. Aureliano becomes Colonel Aureliano Buendía and leads a band of men in the first of seemingly endless civil wars. He fights in thirty-two battles and loses them all. Arcadio dies before a firing squad, screaming these last words: "Long live the Liberal party!"

The beginning and ending of wars are as confusing as such details written in the many history books about nineteenth-century Colombia. When peace is established, Colonel Aureliano Buendía retires, devoting himself to making little gold fish.

The political situation seems to repeat itself in interminable cycles: when there are not rebellions or wars among opposing parties, they arise against the Americans. A United States banana company, unwilling to grant the workers decent working conditions and facilities, provokes a strike. Soldiers massacre thousands of strikers, and then declare nothing happened at all.

Rain inundates Macondo in the sixteenth chapter. It rains for four years, eleven months, and two days. Macondo's previous civilization, along with its materialism and corruption, is wiped away. The town is reborn with an innocence and purity that had been lost.

The total recapturing of this innocent past, however, proves impossible, as is seen in the last four chapters. The family cycle is completed when the child is born with a pig's tail; several references to literature itself create a sense of closure of the book.

A Critical Overview

"Many years later, as he faced the firing squad, Colonel Aureliano Buendía was to remember that distant afternoon when his father took him to discover ice" (11). This is one of the most remarkable opening lines of all Latin American fiction. Much of the excitement about this contemporary literature resides in the way it evokes active participation on the part of the reader. With this sentence García Márquez immediately involves the reader in three aspects of time: the future of "many years later," an assumed present, and the past of "that distant afternoon." Time thus becomes a problematic matter for the reader from the very first line, and will continue being elusive of definition. The reader may ask, for example, "Where does this story really begin?" It could begin within the general framework of the future (starting with the "many years later" and moving forward) or the present or past. Both here and throughout the novel time takes on a certain magical quality that is impossible for the reader to explain totally in rational terms.

In addition to the matter of time, a few intriguing details of a potential plot are set forth in this line. The reader may ask "Will the situation concerning the firing squad be developed or explained?" Given the doubts and uncertainties about the time of events, the reader may question whether this firing squad is just a dramatic device to create immediate suspense, later to be forgotten, or a true indicator of something important to happen. In effect, there will be seven references to this dramatic event in the first four chapters, legitimizing the curiosity aroused in the first line. These references also maintain the suspense. When the colonel finally does face the firing squad, however, in the seventh chapter, he does not die. Rather, his brother saves him at the last moment. The soldiers are so intimidated that they join the two Buendías in their crusade against the Conservatives.

García Márquez's handling of the firing squad event indicates several things about the total novel and the reader's experience of it. Plot suspense in itself is an important aspect of the book. The reader also gains the knowledge and confidence early in the novel that the observation of minute details is a worthwhile task to undertake—this is one of those novels constructed with some type of overall scheme in which details reappear and fit some kind of pattern. Finally, the reader receives an early lesson in doubting and questioning: seven references to a death scene result not in the anticipated murder, but more repetitive action of the sort the reader had already observed.

The matter of "discovering ice" also stands out in this first sentence. It suggests a primitiveness and innocence which surprise the reader yet characterize much of Macondo in the first two chapters. The town, in effect, is a type of biblical paradise where innocence abounds. The narrator explains, still in the first paragraph, that the world "was so recent that many things lacked names, and in order to indicate them it was necessary to point" (11). The Buendía family is still in the process of learning the names of even the most basic things, including ice. This naming of things suggests the act of creation that is so important in the entire novel. The mention of ice in this first sentence, then, has both thematic and structural importance. Thematically, it underlines innocence and creation. In terms of the chapter's structure, the ice becomes the central element in the chapter's organization: from the mention of the ice the narrator moves immediately to Melquíades's other inventions, and then the chapter closes with the actual anecdote of the introduction to the ice. This ending signals several things to the reader. The surprising detail in that first sentence is indeed developed, reaffirming the confidence in the existence of a total pattern suggested by the matter of the firing squad. In addition, the circular structure of the first chapter will be repeated constantly throughout the novel's innumerable inner circles, and in the novel's overall structure, which is also circular.

John S. Brushwood and Seymour Menton have analyzed the opening pages in a fashion similar to that which has been delineated above.[6] Given the elusive nature of *One Hundred Years of Solitude*, it is logical and perhaps instructive about the book to note that one common strategy for its explication has been the selection of key passages for analysis, usually at the beginning or end of the novel. Both the beginning and the ending of this novel are memorable and highly significant pages of the book.

The last three pages reveal several important secrets and change the novel's total experience considerably. Until near the end of the novel few references emphasize the book's status as fiction. It is above all a story of a family and a town, as opposed to a self-referent reflection on fiction. Near the end of the work, nevertheless, García Márquez becomes more playful with his creation, including characters, for example, from the fiction of other writers, such as Carlos Fuentes and Julio Cortázar. In the fifteenth chapter he inserts Lorenzo Gavilán, a character from Fuentes's *The Death of Artemio Cruz*. In the last two chapters there are references to Alvaro, Alfonso, and Germán. They refer to García Márquez's companions from the days at places like the Japy Bar in Barranquilla: Alvaro Cepeda Samudio, Alfonso Fuenmayor, and Germán Vargas (see chapter 1).

The last three pages convert the story of a family and town into a self-conscious fiction. Aureliano discovers the key to deciphering the mysterious parchments that Melquíades had left. The entire family history had been written already: every action throughout the generations had been the fulfillment of the family's destiny. Having been written, it is a fiction, just as is *One Hundred Years of Solitude*. In this way the discovery and experience of Aureliano concerning the fictionality of the Buendía family is parallel to the reader's discovery and experience at the end of the novel. Aureliano isolates himself totally, as an ideal reader, to concentrate on the parchments. He sees the family destiny from those days in Riohacha to the immediate present, with himself living that moment:

Only then did he discover that Amaranta Ursula was not his sister but his aunt, and that Sir Francis Drake had attacked Riohacha only so that they could seek each other through the most intricate labyrinths of blood until they would engender the mythological animal that was to bring the line to an end. (282–83)

The reference to the mythological animal, of course, is the Buendía with the pig's tail that he himself engendered. Reading himself in the text, discovering his own fictionality, he jumps forward to read of the very moment he is living, as reader "prophesying himself in the act of deciphering the last page of parchments, as if he were looking into a speaking mirror" (383). Both Aureliano and the reader not only discover (or are reminded of) the fictionality of the universe of Macondo, but also occupy identical roles at the end, as readers of fiction.[7]

A close look at selected passages such as these allow the analyst to explain some of García Márquez's magic. Some critics have preferred to explain this magic in a more general way, and use the term "magic realism" with respect to this novel. The German art critic Franz Roh first coined the term in 1925 as a magic insight into reality. For Roh it was synonymous with postexpressionist painting (1920–25) because it revealed the mysterious elements hidden in everyday reality. Magic realism expressed man's astonishment before the wonders of the real world; José Arcadio Buendía's amazement over Melquíades's ice is an indication why the term seems appropriate in a discussion of García Márquez.

A writer from the Caribbean region like García Márquez, the Cuban Alejo Carpentier, discussed the "marvelous American reality" in the prologue to his novel *El reino de este mundo* (1949; *The Kingdom of this World,* 1957). For Carpentier, this special reality finds its roots in the marvelous nature of the American cultural experience and history. He proposes there are similarities between this marvelous American reality and poetic epiphany. Several critics of Spanish-American literature popularized the term later, most importantly Angel Flores.[8] Magic realism has been applied to a diverse group of writers and often in reference to any type of writing that portrayed both the real and the fantastic. George McMurray, who defines magic realism as a blend of reality and fantasy, considers *One Hundred Years of Solitude* one of the best examples of magic realism, for both its aesthetic values and universal appeal.[9]

This fusion of the real and the fantastic is present throughout the story. Remedios the Beauty, who functions as a "real" person in the real world of Macondo, suddenly flies into the sky. Perhaps the reader had been prepared by the descriptions of her incredible beauty, which made her something other than human. Characters return from death, such as Melquíades. He is also present even when he is away, and his room stays in immaculate condition even when no one takes care of it. Colonel Aureliano Buendía has seventeen illegitimate sons by seventeen different women. All seventeen are named Aureliano. Thousands of workers are massacred, yet no one besides José Arcadio the labor leader sees or hears of anything: the workers never existed.

One reason that the reader feels the urge to invent a term for all this—such as "magic realism"—is that even the most incredible people, events, or whatever do not really appear as "fantastic." García Márquez prohibits their being fantastic by dealing with them as if they were commonplace. The material for his magic realism, then, is akin to Roh's original idea, relating to everyday life. A clue to the technique of presenting these special things can be found in an anecdote which García Márquez has told concerning his aunt. She seemed to have a knack for convincing others of the truthfulness of her ridiculous explanations for things. When a child once asked her why an egg was shaped so oddly, she answered thoughtfully: "Look, you want to know why this egg has this bulge? Well, because it's a basilisk egg. Light a fire in the patio." Convinced, they built the fire. García Márquez explains that this naturalness was what "gave me the key to *One Hundred Years of Solitude,* in which the most frightful, the most unusual things are told with the same dead-pan expression my aunt had when they burned the basilisk egg on the patio, without ever even knowing what it was."[10]

The nature of reality and the thematic complexity of *One Hundred Years of Solitude* have made it a novel often dealt with in terms of "levels of reality." Critics have discussed numerous levels of reality in this novel, the most common being the social, the historical, the mythical, and the psychological.

At the social level, *One Hundred Years of Solitude* portrays numerous facets of Latin-American society, from class structure to customs. Fernanda represents the aristocratic branch of the family, while Ursula is the person of the "pueblo"—the common folk. The basic customs reflect a provincial and Hispanic tradition. The Catholic church dominates religious life, but religion in general is not an important aspect of everyday life.

At the historical level, the novel can be read as the history of Colombia, the history of Latin America, or even the history of humanity. As a history of each of these entities, Macondo completes an entire cycle: birth, development, prosperity, decadence, and death. At first the town is a prehistoric and primitive society, an idyllic world with even biblical overtones. The first important change takes place when Ursula discovers the route that connects Macondo with the outside world. This could be identified as the point at which Macondo is integrated into history. With its discovery come the first merchants and they will open the first shops. Soon after Macondo receives its first institutions: the government and the church. The arrival of the railroad, electricity, movies, and the telephone give Macondo a face of modernity.

A major historical transformation takes place in Macondo when the American banana company arrives. It becomes a dependent town with a one-product economy. The arrival of an onslaught of outsiders changes the total face of Macondo: the false prosperity and the corruption repeat the scene portrayed in *Leafstorm*. After the company leaves and the bad weather attacks Macondo one more time, the town has exhausted its vitality and completed its last historical cycle.

With respect to the mythical level of reading, *One Hundred Years of Solitude* seems mythlike because so many aspects of the novel are conceived in a way that makes them larger than life. Whether or not such a conception of things is "real" or "possible" is not the matter at hand here. García Márquez has explained his position concerning the importance of myth in his writing:

But I realized that reality is also the myths of the common people, it is the beliefs, their legends; they are their everyday life and they affect their triumphs and failures. I realized that reality isn't just the police that kill people, but also everything that forms part of the life of the common people. All of this must be incorporated. [11]

Colonel Aureliano Buendía, like his historical counterpart Rafael Uribe Uribe, is conceived in this fashion. Each is the result of some actions of which a human being would be capable, and many more that are larger than life, but are perpetrated by the popular image— by what is said, by what is thought, by what is speculated, by gossip. Melquíades is larger-than-life for the inhabitants of Macondo, even though the reader may not be as impressed with his ice and magnets as are the Buendías. His return from death and, at the end, his incredible manuscript, make him a mythic character for the reader too. A character like Ursula is firmly rooted in the world of real life. Nevertheless, her persistence and agelessness place her in the realm of those larger-than-life characters.

The creation of a mythical time contributes to the mythical level of reality. This concept of time negates the lineal progression of normal chronology and history. The Buendías do not make the type of temporal distinctions that history demands: rather, they regularly fail to integrate themselves successfully into the flow of history and civilization. Their actions inevitably reflect a pattern of cyclical repetitions instead of lineal progression. The constant repetitions within the Buendía family, for example, contribute to an experience of an eternal present: the names of the members of the family as well as specific types of personalities. The José Arcadios are physically active and spontaneous, as opposed to the Aurelianos, who tend to be more passive and intellectual in their approach to life. All the actions and events in Macondo eventually appear as the inevitable repetition of probably futile previous actions.

A mythic vision is one way of grasping reality that negates purely rational explanation. The rationality of cause and effect is regularly insufficient in the world of Macondo, from its initial creation in *Leafstorm*. Rather than providing an explanation or interpretation of reality, García Márquez uses myth as a way of preserving and organizing it. Myth integrates a multiplicity of things that are known about and the language through which they are known, and gives them an order which perpetrates their existence. [12]

These levels of reality in the textual fabric, of course, are not mutually exclusive. At times they function simultaneously in a continuous flow; sometimes the different levels find only momentary points of contact. It is possible to construct a reading that combines the mythical and psychological levels. [13] Seen in this way, the structure of *One Hundred Years of Solitude* is based on the Oedipus myth and the Buendía family's genealogical tree. The Oedipus myth of mother-son incest represents a constant threat to societal order in this novel. Observation of the development of the genealogical tree demonstrates both literal and figurative incest. José Arcadio Buendía's marriage with his cousin Ursula is literal incest. His son Aureliano's marriage with Remedios is figurative incest, since he is a metaphoric father because of their age difference. In addition, Rebecca is a figurative sister, being an adopted member of the family. These two bases for the novel's structure, the Oedipus myth and the genealogical tree, when viewed carefully and carried to their ultimate consequences, are mutually exchangeable: the incest of the Oedipus myth pervades the genealogy of the Buendía family and the family's history is constantly determined by incest.

It is entirely possible, given the psychology of incest, for a contemporary writer such as García Márquez to use the myth with no knowledge of its literary antecedents. Incest appears as a deep-seated constant of the human psyche, or an archetype. Other aspects of the novel's universal resonances are more strictly literary.[14] Traditionalists may attempt to prove that García Márquez did indeed read specific books of the Western tradition, and *One Hundred Years of Solitude* is at least partially a product of these readings. Readers and critics less concerned with such scholarly details may be interested in or even intrigued with the parallels between universal writers, whatever the direct or indirect connection between these writers and García Márquez may be. One such literary source for García Márquez is the imaginary biography, a tradition which can be traced from the Bible to the Renaissance, and manifested in modern literature in Virginia Woolf's *Orlando* (1928).[15] In addition to the similarities in the basic novelistic form, *Orlando* and *One Hundred Years of Solitude* share comparable uses of time and satire attitudes about literature.

There are several novels of this type which invite comparison. Borges's first book of fiction, *Historia universal de la infamia* (1935), is a series of short biographies. Like *One Hundred Years of Solitude* and *Orlando,* it is a highly inventive book which, nevertheless, situates the characters in real historical contexts. A similar type of project was Marcel Schwob's *Vies imaginaires* (1896), a book known by Borges, too.

García Márquez's novel has already been described as the story of the people of Macondo; several comparable predecessors of this type of collective story can be pointed out. Daniel Defoe's *A Journal of the Plague Year* tells the story of London during the year of a plague. The well-established link between García Márquez and Faulkner makes most of the latter's fiction a potential source of comparison. Much of Faulkner's work, such as *Absalom, Absalom!,* deals with the collectivity of the family. Many other similarities can be found in the work of the two writers.[16]

The connection between García Márquez and writers such as Borges and Faulkner is a direct one because it is a well-established fact that the Colombian was reading these two during his Barranquilla years (see chapter 1). A discussion of the possible Hispanic origins of *One Hundred Years of Solitude* is more tenuous, but several books demand mention. These include two Spanish classics which are metafictions, Cervantes's *Don Quixote* and Unamuno's *Niebla*. It is notable that the Cuban Alejo Carpentier, whose vision of Latin American reality is defined as "lo maravilloso," published two key novels precisely during García Márquez's period of literary apprenticeship, *El reino de este mundo* (1949) and *Los pasos perdidos* (1953).

One Hundred Years of Solitude is a novel of a strange reality, for the most part readily accessible to read, but elusive to describe or analyze satisfactorily. An awareness of how specific passages function as a part of the whole, its numerous levels of reality, or its literary origins can contribute to a fuller appreciation of its rich possibilities as a reading experience. It is quite likely the best effort in twentieth-century Latin America to create the "total novel," as Vargas Llosa calls it. Perhaps for this reason so many readings of it seem so incomplete.

Social and Political Implications

As the reading of the social and historical levels has suggested, *One Hundred Years of Solitude* abounds in social and political implications. It tells much of the story of social and political life in Colombia and Latin America from the three centuries of the colonial period to the present. Couched in such unreal terms, or portrayed in such seemingly fantastic situations, the social and political sphere easily can be unrecognizable or perhaps ignored by some readers. The foreign reader, enchanted by the book's exotic qualities and perhaps unaware of Latin America's social and political realities, often ignores this aspect.

It could well be that the most appropriate description of Colombia's history is in terms of the fantastic. The conflicts between Liberals and Conservatives in nineteenth-century Colombia did indeed have characteristics of the incredible. Once Macondo is in communication with the rest of the nation, after Ursula's discovery of a route, it lives much of what was Colombia's nineteenth-century history.[17]

Like most Latin American countries, Colombia won its independence from Spain in the early part of the nineteenth century. By 1848 the Liberals and Conservatives were clearly aligned into two parties, with their respective ideological positions defined. The Conservatives were, above all, the supporters of the Catholic church as a powerful institution: they favored the constitutional recognition of the nation as Catholic. The Conservative program favored a powerful executive branch and a centralist as opposed to a federalist government. The Liberals insisted upon a separation of the church and state. They were antichurch in other ways too: they were in favor of freedom of religion, civil marriage, and public education. They demanded absolute freedom of the press, as opposed to what the Conservatives euphemistically called "the responsibility of the press." The Liberals favored a federalist type government, with power given to the different regional governments.

Two constitutions were the basis of political expression and conflict in nineteeth-century Colombia. In 1862 a convention in Rionegro, Antioquia, resulted in the approval of an extremely liberal constitutions that embodied liberal ideals perfectly. This code of laws lasted some twenty years, although not without conflict. In 1884 the Liberal President Rafael Núñez proposed a drastically reformed constitution. The proposal resulted in a division of the Liberal party into two factions—the Independents and the Radicals. The Independents, like the Conservatives, sided with Núñez. He was unable to unify the party; the Radicals broke into an armed revolt in 1885.

One of the leaders in the Radicals' rebellion was General Rafael Uribe Uribe, the prototype for Colonel Aureliano Buendía in *One Hundred Years of Solitude.* After numerous losses on the battlefield, the second constitution was signed in 1886, returning enormous powers to the church and the executive branch of the central government. Dedicated Liberals such as General Uribe Uribe did not take this move lightly. Unfortunately, his determination and tenacity were not matched by his success on the battlefield. He was a national legend by the time he ended his eighteen-year struggle in defense of Liberal ideals—losing most if not all his battles—by signing the Treaty of Neerlandia in 1902. This treaty put an end to this lengthy conflict, the War of a Thousand Days, which lasted from 1899 to 1902. General Uribe Uribe's heroic and often spontaneous call for battle was quite similar to Aureliano Buendía's behavior in the novel.

Several other direct similarities can be noted between General Uribe Uribe and Colonel Aureliano Buendía.[18] When faced with possible death, both of them attempted to flee from the government, Uribe Uribe at the end of a second war, Buendía after Macondo's first war. They both suffered in jail, but both were extraordinarily durable. Both mounted campaigns to gain support from abroad. In the end, Colonel Aureliano Buendía embodies not only the popular legend of General Uribe Uribe, but also the entire history of the Liberals during this period. It was a history of heroic ideals and acts, and consistent defeat.

During the same period, the end of the nineteenth century, another important historical event was taking place, the entrance of the United Fruit Company into Colombia. At the end of the century, bananas were produced by two companies, the Colombia Land Company and the Boston Fruit Company. A merger in 1899 resulted in the formation of United Fruit. The American company also purchased bananas from Colombian companies. The railway to the port city of Santa Marta was completed in 1906, so fruit was transported there to be shipped to American ports. The changes in the local economy and social-political structure related in *One Hundred Years of Solitude* with the arrival of Mr. Herbert are parallel, then, to the transformation that did take place at the beginning of the twentieth century in the coastal region of Colombia.

In November of 1928 a strike was declared in the area. The workers for the United Fruit Company made a series of demands, mostly related to working conditions. The demands included the social security guaranteed by Colombian law, compliance with laws protecting workers in accidents, fulfillment of laws concerning housing, the right to commerce instead of company stores, and the building of hospitals. The list of demands that the workers present in the novel is basically the same.

The solution to this conflict is identical in the historical and fictional accounts. First, the striking workers were declared "nonexistent." Technically speaking, the company classified them as part-time employees, thus avoiding the legal obligations that apply only to full-time workers. Faced with a physical confrontation, the army massacred the strikers. The different history books vary in the exact number of workers who died, as do other accounts written at the time. A telegram sent by the United States ambassador from Colombia to the State Department indicated that the number of deaths was in excess of a thousand. In the novel, as well as in this region at the time, there was absolute silence concerning the massacre: no one dared speak of the horrible events, fearing repression.

It is important to note, within the context of Colombia's history, that the phenomenon of banana exploitation and the resultant confrontation were not typical of Colombia's economic history, as the country's economic base has not been an export economy in the control of foreign capitalists.[19] Many Latin American countries have been dominated by this type of economy, but Colombia has relied primarily on coffee production, owned and operated by nationals. García Márquez's special vision in *One Hundred Years of Solitude,* markedly anticapitalist, has evolved around a series of circumstances quite different from the standard situation in Colombia. The export economy and confrontation presented in the novel thus may be seen as an ideologeme for a pattern common throughout Latin American history as a whole. Many Latin American countries have had or presently do have basically export economies controlled by foreign capitalists.

Other ideologemes function to communicate at the level of social or political reality. The endless repetition of useless actions are an ideologeme for a capitalist society without social or economic vitality. In this sense the colonel's endless battles are the same as his repetitive creation of little gold fish: they both present a paradigm of action for the sake of action (or production for the sake of production), with no worthwhile return. Macondo never functions as an authentic participant in the political and economic processes of the nation. It is always marginal at best. Even after establishing his government position in Macondo, Moscote is nothing more than an "ornamental" authority, as he is described in the text. National politics are more a matter of disruption or confusion than an integral part of Macondo's life. After painting and repainting their homes the colors of both the Liberals and the Conservatives, Macondo's citizens eventually have houses of an undefined color, a sign of the failure, in effect, of both traditional parties.

One Hundred Years of Solitude is a unique social document in that it captures a wide gamut of Colombia's social, political, and economic realities. For Colombia, it is anomalous in its portrayal of the social and political consequences of the export economy that was in existence for only a short period in a small region in Colombia. It is a paradigm that applies, however, to much of Latin America and parts of the Third World. At the same time García Márquez portrays the central conflict between Colombia's traditional political and economic sectors, the civil wars between Liberals and Conservatives. His method for fictionalizing this conflict is to characterize the most vividly remembered legendary figure of this period. For his most historically based material, García Márquez has chosen two vastly different types of situations; in fictionalizing them he has masterfully captured the essence of both Colombian and Latin-American social and political realities.

Narrative Technique and Universality

"Art is not a copy of the real world. One of the damn things is enough." That is one art critic's view of artistic creation, and possibly a worthwhile point of departure in a general discussion of García Márquez. *One Hundred Years of Solitude* certainly does relate in numerous ways to the real world of Latin America and even Western civilization, as has been demonstrated in this chapter. This fact in itself, however, is a very incomplete description of the novel, since all art, in one way or another, relates in some way to the real world. Equally incomplete, then, are the readings that attempt to reduce *One Hundred Years of Solitude* to just a social document. A fuller understanding and appreciation of the novel is possible through an analysis of narrative techniques and the dynamics of reading.

García Márquez's previous fiction was, in a certain way, an apprenticeship in the use of narrative techniques. A variety of techniques to create humor is evident in *Leafstorm,* some of the stories of *Big Mama's Funeral,* and *No One Writes to the Colonel.* In stories as early as "The Other Side of Death" the young writer was experimenting with techniques that would create special effects with time. Much of his previous fiction, particularly the initial stories and *Leafstorm,* were experiments with techniques that might create the sensation of some "other reality," different from our everyday reality of cause and effect. In the previous fiction García Márquez experimented with virtually all imaginable uses of narrative point of view, sometimes employing more than one narrative voice in the same story. Many of these techniques, from the humor to the special effects achieved from uses of narrative point of view, were exploited with some success in the earlier fiction. They are perfected with the writing of *One Hundred Years of Solitude.*

García Márquez claims to have discovered the key to handling the narrative voice in this novel when he remembered how his grandmother used to tell him stories. His revelation was that he should tell his story as she told hers.[20] This anecdote could well be true, but it is quite a simplification. Technically speaking, the narrator in the novel is third-person omniscient. This narrator does occasionally reveal what the characters think. The predominant mode, however, is external: the reader observes the characters act and speak.

The narrator is detached from what he narrates—he offers a seemingly neutral understanding and presentation of the fictional world. Certain nuances betray total neutrality. On the one hand, the narrator often functions as if he were a character in the novel. At times he demonstrates an innocence or amazement with the world similar to the characters. The narrator thinks like them, demonstrating at times the same prejudices, at others the same primitiveness of the people of Macondo.

One consistently used technique, also similar to the views of the people of Macondo, is an absolute coolness or understatement when describing the incredible situations, and overstatement or exaggeration when dealing with the commonplace. In the ice episode in the first chapter, for example, the narrator's language shares the characters' exaggerated reaction to Melquíades's new object. At first, José Arcadio Buendía calls it "el diamante más grande del mundo" (23) ("the largest diamond in the world," 26). The narrator uses language that is similar to José Arcadio's a few lines later: "el corazón se le hinchaba de temor y de júbilo al contacto del misterio" (23) ("his heart filled with fear and jubilation at the contact with mystery," 26). He has his children live this "prodigiosa experiencia," in the words of the narrator. By the end of the episode the narrator has used the words "misterioso," "prodigioso," and "embriagador" to describe what would seem to the readers the most commonplace of everyday experiences, touching ice. Similarly, the narrator describes the magnets which Melquíades brings to Macondo as "la octava maravilla de los sabios alquimistas de Macedonia" (9). The narrator, like the characters, regularly expresses his astonishment over the commonplace.

In contrast, he regularly reacts to the most marvelous and fantastic things with absolute passivity—the lesson in technique learned from his grandmother. In the same first chapter José Arcadio and his children experience the disappearance of a man who becomes invisible after drinking a special potion (22). Neither the narrator nor the characters pay particular attention to this incredible occurrence. There are only rare exceptions to the narrator's basic position of third-person omniscience. The entire issue of the narrator undergoes a radical change at the end of the novel when it is revealed that in reality the narrator of the entire story was Melquíades. The magician of Macondo has also been the creator of magic for the reader. Suddenly the reader comes to the realization that the narrator is not outside the story but within. This discovery underscores the story's basic fictionality, another fact which might have been momentarily forgotten by the reader, absorbed in this history of Colombia and saga of Western civilization. Another exception to the narrator's basic position of third-person omniscience occurs in chapter 16 when Fernanda creates an extensive monologue (274–76). It could be seen as a dialogue too, with her diatribe being directed to Aureliano Segundo.

The narrator's special position as both teller of the story and character in Macondo provides for an ample integration of different languages in the text—the phenomenon of heteroglossia.[21] One reason many readers consider *One Hundred Years of Solitude* a "total" novel resides in the fact that the panoply of different languages creates numerous resonances. Resonances of biblical language, for example, contribute to the reading of the novel as a total history of mankind since the creation, or Genesis. The narrator incorporates languages that have the resonance of distinct historical periods, each of which also contribute to the book's universal overtones. The narrator, for example, employs a language associated with the Middle Ages when he describes José Arcadio Buendía attacking Prudencio Aguilar as a "duel of honor" (30). He uses an equally antiquated and anachronistically humorous language to describe Rebecca's reaction to the masculine qualities of José Arcadio. In this case the original Spanish is more sexist in language, describing him as a "protomacho": "La tarde en que lo vio pasar frente a su dormitorio pensó que Pietro Crespi era un currutaco de alfeñique junto a aquel protomacho cuya respiración volcánica se percibía en toda la casa" (85) ("The day that she saw him pass by her bedroom she thought that Pietro Crespi was a sugary dandy next to that protomale whose volcanic breathing could be heard all over the house," 94).

The insomnia plague of the third chapter threatens the loss of language, a potential elimination of all the layers of heteroglossia that saturate the consciousness of Macondo. The insomnia reduces linguistic expression to the recognition of only the most basic objects. A sign is placed at the entrance to the town which reads "Macondo" to assure the preservation of the town's identity. More important, with respect to the novel's heteroglossia, is the larger sign placed in Macondo's main street: "God exists." The one language they choose to preserve, beyond that of everyday objects, is religious language. This act has numerous connotations; among them, the reader is reminded of the numerous languages that have been forgotten or eliminated in societies like Macondo's. For example, no effort is made to preserve the language of the Enlightenment. Macondo's society seems to systematically preserve the languages of conservatism or even repression, and eliminate the vocabulary of progress or revolution. The striking workers' words of protest have been forgotten in another insomniac-type process: no written signs remain in Macondo to preserve their list of demands, for example.

García Márquez incorporates languages of different types of literature, including the specific novels already discussed in this chapter. This can include parody, such as the anecdote of the soldier who falls in love with Remedios the Beauty. The ninth chapter ends with the following description of the outcome of this love: "El Día de Año Nuevo, enloquecido por los desaires de Remedios, la bella, el joven comandante de la guardia amaneció muerto de amor junto a su ventana" (158). The original Spanish has him "dead of love," whereas the published translation loses some of the melodrama: "On New Year's Day, driven mad by rebuffs from Remedios the Beauty, the young commander of the guard was found dead under her window" (173). Read in the original, and with a knowledge of the Latin-American novelistic tradition, this passage is a humorous parody of Latin America's ostentatiously melodramatic tradition of romantic literature. The best known of these, still read today in the Hispanic world, is the Colombian Jorge Isaacs's *María* (1867).

Some readers might not be aware of a parody such as this. Generally speaking, however, *One Hundred Years of Solitude* is a supremely well calculated book with respect to that most important element of all fiction—the reader. García Márquez's career as a journalist not only allowed the opportunity, but absolutely demanded an awareness of the reader. His entertaining "Relato de un náufrago" was important in this respect (see chapter 2). One critic has even suggested that *One Hundred Years of Solitude* is an "extended accolade to the reader."[22] First, it has those elements most basic to maintaining reader interest: an interesting plot and action. Wayne Booth has proposed that fiction may offer the reader three kinds of values of interest:[23] (1) intellectual or cognitive: an intellectual curiosity about "the facts"; (2) qualitative: a desire to see any pattern or form completed; and (3) practical: a desire for the success or failure of those we love or hate, or the hope or fear of a change in the quality of a character. García Márquez successfully manipulates all three of these potential interests. Different readers, with different interests, could be equally attracted to the intellectual or cognitive discovery of the historical and political reading, the qualitative interest involved with the cyclical and other patterns, or the practical interests related to many of the individual characters.

When a novel seems to do everything, it is not surprising that it also shows how to read. In the first chapter José Arcadio Buendía is the master of reading, teaching this art to his sons. In this chapter, reading is not merely a passive intellectual exercise, but an adventure in invention and the imagination. From this exciting discovery forward the reader enjoys a most privileged position in the text: receiving intellectual, qualitative, and practical values; enjoying a superior position with respect to Macondo's characters, and being able to laugh at their idiosyncracies. At the end the reader is especially privileged, having a knowledge of the family vastly superior to that of its last members, and sharing with Aureliano Babilonia a very special manuscript. The reader who has completed this manuscript, like this ideal reader Aureliano, is both a clever decipherer of textual clues and possessor of a vast knowledge of the universe. García Márquez has fictionalized a reader whose role the real reader is charmed and honored to play.

One Hundred Years of Solitude obviously communicates a panoply of experiences to a vast range of readers. His techniques for involving the reader and creating a total fictional universe make the novel highly experiential: the reading experience itself, the process, is as important as the intellectualization that often follows an actual reading. Seen in retrospect, after the reading, the novel contains that same basic affirmation in mankind noted in many of his previous stories. It is an affirmation based on an underlying, but constant, respect for the plight of the common man. This fundamental optimism is not found necessarily in individual or collective triumphs over the immediate social circumstance, but in a faith that the human spirit will allow all humans to prevail with dignity, whatever the forces in opposition may be. From the hilarious creations of José Arcadio Buendía in the first chapter to the magnificent creation of Melquíades in the last, *One Hundred Years of Solitude* is living proof of the proposition that "By creation, then, Creation is celebrated."

Chapter Five
The Incredible and Sad Tale of Innocent Eréndira and Her Heartless Grandmother (1972)

Introduction

The stories in this volume are, above all, entertainments. Written between 1968 and 1972, with the exception of one story, they are the product of a writer who obviously takes pleasure in both writing and entertaining; during this period, perhaps more than any, García Márquez could enjoy the luxury of doing what he does best, writing good stories.

The overwhelming impact of the Spanish edition of *One Hundred Years of Solitude* in 1967 produced what could be called the "phenomenon of Macondo" in Colombia and the Spanish-speaking world.[1] It was a phenomenon that García Márquez had partially created himself with the publication of the novel. Whatever its multiple causes, it was not something which he could ignore. On the one hand, the phenomenon was an expression of the popularity of the novel and García Márquez as its creator. This involved the continental fascination with Macondo, sales of books, innumerable interviews, and journalistic commentary on matters relating to the work and the author, and, of course, his politics. On the other hand, there were factors beyond his control, above all, the criticism. Few, if any, Latin-American novels had ever inspired so much critical attention, including that from American academia with its constant flow of doctoral dissertations. The novel also happened to coincide with the upsurge in international interest in literary theory. The results of this vast critical enterprise on García Márquez have been uneven, ranging from the lucid to the absurd, from informative to incomprehensible. If the culminating book in García Márquez's career was *One Hundred Years of Solitude,* the equally culminating work of the phenomenon of Macondo, at least in the Hispanic world, was Mario Vargas Llosa's 667-page study, *Gabriel García Márquez: historia de un deicidio* (1971). García Márquez himself, who has never had any pretense of being either a critic or scholar of literature, has remained for the most part distanced and sometimes vocally skeptical about the vast critical enterprise, including that which has arisen around his own work.

García Márquez's attitude vis-à-vis literary critics has at least some logical roots. The fact that much of the reaction in the Hispanic world has been articulated by journalists, quite often in search of only the momentary scandal or outrage, has made García Márquez understandably cautious. At the other extreme, the highly specialized and often esoteric studies published by foreign academics probably seem as remote to García Márquez as would daily life in Aracataca or the music of the coastal *vallenato* to the ivory-tower scholar.

More important, with respect to García Márquez the writer, however, is the antirationalist mode of thought that permeates all of his fiction, from the first stories to *One Hundred Years of Solitude.* They reflect an underlying lack of confidence in man's rational capacities. García Márquez constantly convinces or reminds his readers that rational processes are just one fact in human understanding and conception of reality. The stories in this volume express this antirationalist tendency. In addition, they are a reaction to the phenomenon of Macondo, both *One Hundred Years of Solitude* and the critical apparatus that surrounds it.

"A Very Old Man with Enormous Wings" and "The Handsomest Drowned Man in the World"

The presence of "A Very Old Man with Enormous Wings" as the first story of the volume is absolutely fundamental to the book's total experience.[2] It establishes certain themes and makes an important initial step in the fictionalization of a reader. This story and "The Handsomest Drowned Man in the World" are entertaining treatments of one of the matters that became so important with the publication of *One Hundred Years of Solitude:* interpretation.

The setting for "A Very Old Man with Enormous Wings" is a poor coastal village. Pelayo and his wife Elisenda are the central characters. One day Pelayo goes to dispose of crabs washed ashore and discovers a strange being of human form: an old man with wings, lying face down in the muddy beach. The hapless winged man is toothless, bald, and dressed in rags. Pelayo and Elisenda examine the creature carefully, looking for clues to its possible genre or origin. The unknown man responds to their queries in a foreign tongue which they cannot identify. They suspect he is a castaway from a ship. Other inhabitants of the town observe the old man and offer several possible explanations for his origin. They plan to send him afloat, on a raft, but first imprison him in a chicken coop.

It soon becomes apparent that there is too much interest in this creature to justify his abandonment: a large crowd congregates at the chicken coop for a glance at the being rumored to be an angel. The whole matter has the air of a circus, especially when Elisenda decides to charge admission to see him. They simply do not know what to do with him. There are several suggestions, such as naming him the mayor of the world and making him a five-star general. The winged man does not respond to any of these ideas.

Father Gonzaga pays the man a visit to ascertain any possible filiation with angels. The fact that the potential angel does not seem to know Latin places his sanctity in serious question and even suggests that he could be associated with the devil. The priest sends a letter to the pope, requesting a definitive clarification. The response from Rome is not helpful: the Vatican only asks more questions, wanting to know, for example, if the creature has a navel. Even the possibility of divine origin is enough to sustain the belief in the town that the old man might have the ability to perform miracles. A horde of the sick and handicapped throng to his side in search of a cure. The results are not the desired ones, although the man does seem to have some effect on the hopeful: a blind man, for example, grows new teeth.

García Márquez presents a distraction to this story line with the introduction of a special woman who arrives at the town with her traveling show. She has been transformed into a spider for having disobeyed her parents. The town's inhabitants become more interested in this marvelous woman than in the old man.

Pelayo and Elisenda, nevertheless, already have profited well from their prisoner. They have built a fancy home and Elisenda boasts the finest wardrobe in town. The old man is moved into their home after his chicken coop collapses. One morning while she is performing her regular daily chores, she sees him begin to flap his wings.

She watches him fly off to "Un punto imaginario en el horizonte del mar"[3] ("an imaginary dot on the horizon of the sea").[4]

The most important concern established in this first story of the volume is interpretation. Upon the discovery of the stranger, six interpretations arise within the story. After Pelayo recovers from his initial astonishment, he arrives at the conclusion that the unknown man is a "náufago solitario" ("lonely castaway"). The basis for this conclusion is that he speaks with a "strong sailor's voice." The reader considers this explanation arbitrary: basic logic rejects this explanation and Pelayo's idea is humorous. The second interpretation is made by a neighbor whom everyone considers very knowledgeable. According to the narrator, she knows "everything about life and death." The humor of her interpretation resides in her modus operandi: "all she needed was one look to show them their mistake." Then she declares rotundly: "It is an angel." The reader laughs at her affirmation because of the contrast between the absurdity of the interpretation and the absolute confidence with which she manifests it.

The next three interpretations are proposed by the innocent and ingenuous inhabitants of the town. He could be, according to them, the mayor of the world, a five-star general, or the first of a "race of winged wise men who could take charge of the universe." Father González offers the sixth interpretation upon concluding that the man is not an angel. It is notable that the "official" interpreter in the town, the priest, is the only one who refuses to offer any concrete or definitive interpretation: he sends a letter to Rome instead.

The text offers no rational explanation for the enigmatic man. It is suggested that he is just imaginary, since he disappears in "an imaginary dot on the horizon of the sea." "A Very Old Man with Enormous Wings" is a parody of the interpretive process. It could even be seen as a reaction to the critical and interpretive machinery which arose after the publication of *One Hundred Years of Solitude,* during the period these stories were written. Appearing as the first story in the volume, it also functions as a type of warning to the reader: one must take extreme care in attributing rational laws of cause and effect on innately irrational things. The story also affirms García Márquez's right of invention. The final line makes this affirmation, as well as a pair of highly inventive diversions from the basic story line. The first is a hyperbolic description of certain individuals who come to see the fallen angel:

The curious came from far away. A traveling carnival arrived with a flying acrobat who buzzed over the crowd several times, but no one paid any attention to him because his wings were not those of an angel, but, rather, those of a sidereal bat. The most unfortunate invalids on earth came in search of health: a poor woman who since childhood had been counting her heartbeats and had run out of numbers; a Portuguese man who couldn't sleep because the noise of the stars disturbed him; a sleepwalker who got up at night to undo the things he had done while awake; and many with less serious ailments. (161)

The second inventive diversion occurs when the woman converted into a spider arrives in town. A ray of lightning had stricken her when she was returning home late at night after going to a dance without her parents' permission. Her only food was little balls of ground meat that kind souls threw to her. This incredible story distracts both the inhabitants and the reader from the old man's predicament.

This story is narrated by an omniscient narrator outside the story. Some slight variations have the effect of communicating some events from the point of view of the town's inhabitants. In the story's first paragraph, in which Pelayo collects the errant crabs, the perspective already reflects him. When the narrator states, for example, "El cielo y el mar eran una misma cosa de ceniza" ("Sea and sky were a single ash-gray thing"), this language and view reflect Pelayo's vision of things. Soon thereafter, Pelayo and Elisenda observe the old man lying on the beach and the narrator states: "Estaba vestido como un trapero" (11) ("He was dressed like a ragpicker," 158). The pair, rather than strictly the narrator, are viewing the man as a ragpicker. Such descriptions are effective, and humorous, precisely because of the prosaic ways the characters perceive things. Similarly, when the narrator states that the neighbor knows "everything about life and death," this is really the popular belief, the language of the townsfolk in general. The story vacillates between two basic perspectives, that of the distant omniscient narrator, and that of the people of the town, as individuals or as a collectivity.

The reader fictionalized in this story occupies a position superior to these characters who view odd persons as clowns and believe that their neighbors can possess supernatural powers. This superiority is important for the story's humor, but is only a minor aspect of the reader's total characterization. Two more significant aspects are the reader's attitude vis-à-vis invention and interpretation. The reader fictionalized in the text appreciates invention in itself and learns to accept its privileged function in this story. The two imaginative diversions from the main story line gives invention precedence over action or finality. The reader approaches interpretation with extreme caution: attributing symbolic value to either the old man or his inexplicable final act probably will be just one more act of pointless interpretation.

The reader fictionalized in "The Handsomest Drowned Man in the World" occupies a similar position. The basic situation in the story is identical: a foreign element arrives in a town, inexplicably, and interrupts the regular everyday order. In this case the foreigner is the corpse of a drowned man who has a surprisingly strong impact on the town. Some children on the beach discover the corpse as it floats ashore. They innocently play with him in the sand, burying and unburying the body. When adults discover these games, they are horrified; men carry the body to the nearest house. They note that he is larger and heavier than normal. In fact, the corpse is so covered with a crust of mud and scales that he hardly seems human.

The townfolk soon discover his physical makeup even more impressive than his unorthodox arrival. The women scrape ocean debris off his body, and clean him to find a most impressive human specimen: he is the tallest, strongest, handsomest, and best-endowed male they have ever seen. They fantasize about the man to such an extent that they secretly despise their own men. They uniformly agree that his name must be Esteban.

Then the men of the town, who had gone to nearby towns in search of the man's origins, return with the news that he belongs to no one. The women rejoice, concluding that now he can be considered truly theirs. They organize a splendid funeral for him, even assigning various persons roles as members of the family so he will not have to be buried as an orphan. Esteban's departure creates an awareness of the emptiness of their own lives. For the first time the people realize how empty their streets are and how sterile their lives have been. They believe, however, that things will change: from the size of the buildings in the town to the flowers that will be cultivated, everything will be better in the town.

This story is more clearly developed and affirmative than "A Very Old Man with Enormous Wings." The ending suggests that change is possible and a key to progress is one's attitude. By using resources

available to all human beings—such as imagination—the inhabitants discover that life has seemingly limitless possibilities.
The problem of interpretation arises as soon as the children see
the corpse floating in the distance. At first they think it is an enemy
ship. Their second interpretation is that it is a whale. Soon they
postulate that his size is due to the fact that certain drowned persons
keep growing after death. The townspeople elaborate the interpre-
tative process considerably, attributing supernatural powers to the
man. They believe, for example, that the ocean has never been as
rough as that night when the drowned man was at sea.

These explanations, just like the numerous interpretations of the
winged man's presence in the previous story, are rejected by the
reader. They place into question the possibilities and limits of man's
rational understanding of the world. Both stories demand that the
reader approach interpretation—and the process of reading these
stories—with an awareness of the problem of interpretation and the
limits of one's strictly rational faculties.

These two stories are significant in other ways within the context
of García Márquez's total writing career. They appear after *One
Hundred Years of Solitude* and represent García Márquez's successful
move beyond Macondo, both as a physical setting and as a fictional
world. His imagination was evident in all the work of the Macondo
cycle; now imagination is a theme in itself. Naturally, there are
similarities in narrative technique: as in some of the earlier stories,
García Márquez uses the foreign element which interrupts the everyday order of things as a point of departure in fiction.

One indicator of the readings these stories allow—in support of
what has been proposed already concerning interpretation—is the
fact that these are children's stories.[5] When they are read this way,
no elaborate interpretive scheme is necessary or even appropriate,
for example, for the spider's presence in the first story: it is an
imaginative and entertaining lesson in what can happen to children
who disobey their parents. As children's stories, they need no defense
for being entertainments.

"The Sea of Lost Time" and
"Blacaman the Good, Vendor of Miracles"

Imagination is a theme in this volume and is especially important
in these two stories. They are stories of unrestrained invention and

miraculous happenings. Their similarities are more coincidental than directly historical: "The Sea of Lost Time" (1961) is the only story of the volume written before the publication of *One Hundred Years of Solitude,* whereas "Blacaman the Good, Vendor of Miracles" (1968) is a post-Macondo product.

"The Sea of Lost Time," like much of the Macondo literature, begins with several enigmatic references that will be clarified later in the story. During the month of January the sea became "harsh" and garbage from it, along with its odors, spread over the small town that is the story's setting. Oddly, the smell is of roses. Tobías smells the strong odors first and discusses the matter with his wife Clotilde and the town's inhabitants. An older inhabitant, Petra, views the strange events as a sign of her imminent death. She tells her husband Jacob that, in order to be assured of being buried underground, she wishes to be buried alive. When she does die, nevertheless, she is thrown into the sea. Tobías smells the special odor again, and it eventually inundates the entire town. It causes outsiders to come to see this strange town.

A change takes place when Mr. Herbert, an American, arrives. He announces that he is the richest man in the world: he has so much money that he does not know where to put it and has a heart so big it will not fit in his chest. Mr. Herbert claims to possess the fairest system known to distribute wealth. His first example is a boy who needs forty-eight pesos. The American has him imitate forty-eight birds to earn his money. A girl who needs five-hundred pesos, and who sells herself for five pesos per man, finds Mr. Herbert willing to pay a hundred men to sleep with her. By playing checkers with Jacob, Mr. Herbert wins all his belongings from him, including his home. The American wins other houses. Then he declares a week of festivities and promises an exciting future for the town, which will have glass buildings. He does not initiate construction, however, but just sleeps for days. Eventually the smell of roses disappears, as do the visitors to the town.

At the end of the story, Mr. Herbert takes Tobías for a trip to the bottom of the sea. Tobías sees a new and magnificent world populated with people riding horses on kiosks and giant turtles, among other wonders. When they return from their trip, Mr. Herbert explains to Tobías that he should tell no one of what he has seen, for there would be terrible disorder in the world if everyone knew of such things. Tobías does attempt to relate the story to

Clotilde, but she has no interest in his story of a town with little white houses and millions of flowers on the terraces.

The presence of Mr. Herbert provides a paradigm for exploitative situations similar to the literature of Macondo to which this story more appropriately belongs. The American's token gifts, false goodwill, promises for a splendid future, and acquisition of the town's property are all characteristic of the manipulations of foreign capitalists in the earlier fiction. More important, García Márquez is concerned with imagination and its role in liberation. The only person able to conceive of a world other than this one of subservience and exploitation is Tobías, who literally sees other possibilites, a fantasy world vastly superior to his own. The key sentence is Mr. Herbert's admonition: "Imagínate el desorden que habría en el mundo si la gente se enterara de estas cosas" (44) ("Just imagine the disorder there'd be in the world if people found out about these things," 80). Knowledge of other worlds, even in the form of fantasy, represents an enormous threat to the maintenance of the status quo.

A paradigm of exploitation and liberation is set forth also in "Blacaman the Good, Vendor of Miracles." The two characters, Blacaman the Good and Blacaman the Bad, are in a relationship with each other and among others which always involves a type of exploitation. The development of the situation allows for rich invention.

The narrator of the story, Blacaman the Good, tells his own story and that of his original master, Blacaman the Bad. The latter is a confidence man and charlatan, vendor of anything the foolish or innocent people in the small towns of La Guajira are willing to buy. The story's first paragraph (an extensive anecdote of two and one half pages), provides an entertaining introductory characterization of Blacaman the Bad. He is seen selling his antidote for snake bites to the naive townspeople who observe his show. Dressed in gaudy clothes, covered with bright colors and flashy jewelry, he demonstrates his medicine's effectiveness by faking a snake bite, rolling on the ground in supposed pain, and then recovering miraculously with his special potion. The event was so impressive, according to the narrator, that the marines took color pictures with long-distance lenses. The impressed townsfolk rush to buy their bottles of the medicine, and even the admiral of the American ship decides to purchase some.

The pair has to flee from pursuing marines after the admiral who had purchased the antidote dies from it. In the process, the marines also kill the "natives as a precaution . . . the Chinese for distraction . . . the Blacks out of habit . . ." and "the Hindi for being snake charmers . . ." (88). The two magicians hide in a colonial mission. Blacaman the Bad tortures the narrator sadistically, hanging him by his ankles in the sun and pulling out his fingernails. The narrator finally reacts, throwing a dead rabbit against a wall. From the moment the rabbit returns to life and walks back to him, he is endowed with magical powers.

The narrator, who identifies himself as Blacaman the Good, has a radically different life from the moment he acquires special powers. He leaves his master and becomes a famous miracle healer. His abilities make him so successful that he becomes a rich capitalist with a private chauffeur. Blacaman the Bad eventually reappears, old and decrepit. The narrator's former teacher dies from one of his own medicines, in public, and Blacaman the Good makes no attempt to save him. The narrator's final revenge is to bring his ex-master from death only to make him live in his own tomb for eternity.

Beyond observing the paradigm for exploitation and liberation, interpretation of this story is complicated by several factors. The use of a first-person narrator makes any definitive statement about either of the Blacamans most questionable. At the outset the younger Blacaman seems respectable and a reliable source of information. His rise to fame, however, reveals him to be perhaps as much a charlatan as his teacher. The fact that he identifies himself as an "artist" (92) places into question the accuracy of his story.

It could well be that the best sign of the narrator's successful manipulation of magic and his observer's perceptions is his persuasion of the reader that he indeed is Blacaman *the Good*.[6] The first step in the manipulation of the reader is the initial characterization of Blacaman the Bad as the slick operator before an innocent public as opposed to the equally innocent narrator with his "cara de bobo." The reader will naturally sympathize with the exploited over the exploiter. Only the distant and cautious reader, perhaps remembering the lessons learned in those initial stories concerning the intricacies of interpretation, will maintain a skeptical attitude with respect to the Blacaman that narrates.

A technical innovation in this story is the use of dialogue within sentences with no punctuation to distinguish between the narrator's

words and those of the other speakers. In several of the stories in
this volume García Márquez has used the language and perspective
of the characters described, a narrative position quite close to the
one described here. He uses this technique at the end of the first
sentence:

Desde el primer domingo que lo vi me pareció una mula de monosabio
. . . sólo que entonces no estaba tratando de vender nada a aquella co-
chambre de indios, sino pidiendo que le llevaran una culebra de verdad
para demostrar en carne propia un contraveneno de su invención, el único
indeleble, señoras y señores, contra las picaduras de serpientes, tarántulas
y escolopendras, y toda clase de mamíferos ponzoñosos. (83)

From the first Sunday I saw him he reminded me of a bullring mule, . . .
except that at that time he wasn't trying to sell any of that Indian mess
but was asking him to bring him a real snake so that he could demonstrate
on his own flesh an antidote he had invented, the only infallible one,
ladies and gentlemen, for the bites of serpents, tarantulas, and centipedes
plus all manner of poisonous mammals.[7]

The sentence is a direct quote of Blacaman the Bad's words from
"señoras y señores" forward, even though there are no quotation
marks. This technique is particularly effective and appropriate because the vendor's spoken words themselves are a fundamental part
of his total show. By incorporating this oral language with the
narration of his acts, García Márquez subtly blends word and act—
precisely the effect Blacaman himself wishes to achieve with his
show.
  This technique, which the author uses throughout the story, also
marks the beginning of a new direction in García Márquez's writing.
The long paragraphs and intercalation of dialogue within sentences
will be more fully developed techniques in *The Autumn of the Patriarch*. Three other stories in this volume point to the later novel:
"Innocent Eréndira," "The Last Voyage of the Ghost Ship," and
"Death Constant Beyond Love."

"The Incredible and Sad Tale of Innocent Eréndira and Her Heartless Grandmother," "The Last Voyage of the Ghost Ship," and "Death Constant Beyond Love"

At the outset of this chapter it was pointed out that the first
story in this Spanish edition, "The Handsomest Drowned Man in

the World," is absolutely fundamental to an understanding and full appreciation of the remainder of the stories in the volume. Of course, this and the other stories of this 1968–72 period can be read in an isolated fashion and still be considered worthy. Such is the case of "The Incredible and Sad Tale of Innocent Eréndira and Her Heartless Grandmother": if one reads it as the last story of the total volume, it contains elements of play which are lost in an isolated reading, or the reading offered in the first edition in English.[8] The reason for this is that numerous characters from the other stories reappear in this last story of the volume. The title story thus points back to the previous fiction of this period, and forward to the next novel because of its thematic content.

"Innocent Eréndira" tells the story of an adolescent girl who is cruelly exploited by her grandmother. Its sixty-six pages are divided into seven sections. In the beginning, Eréndira functions as the housekeeper and slave in the grandmother's home. The grandmother's deceased husband, Amadís, was the father of the Amadís who fathered Eréndira. Beyond these basic facts, the details of the family background are unclear, but it is said among the townsfolk that both of Eréndira's parents are dead. The granddaughter performs her numerous tasks in the household efficiently and, given the burden, stoically.

Eréndira's life takes an irrevocable turn for the worse for a reason beyond her control. One night the wind blows over the candelabra in the girl's room, resulting in a fire that destroys the house and all the grandmother's belongings. The grandmother declares that Eréndira must repay every cent, and begins to sell her as a fourteen-year-old prostitute. At first the grandmother obtains a maximum price for her virginity, and then forces the girl to perform an incredible number of sexual acts for the long line of men who wait for her services. After six months of the girl's labor, the grandmother calculates that, at the present rate, the girl will need to work for eight years, seven months, and eleven days to cancel her debt.

The first change in Eréndira's life takes place when she meets Ulises, the son of a Dutch farmer and an Indian. The father and son stop at the tent where they see a line of soldiers awaiting their turn with Eréndira. The grandmother allows the exhausted and sickly girl to have part of the night for rest after performing for numerous soldiers. Ulises, who had heard of the girl's legendary beauty, visits her at night. They fall in love. For the first time she begins to imagine a life other than one of ugliness and exploitation.

Eréndira's life changes radically when she is kidnapped by nuns who place her in their convent. She not only learns a new way of living, but is happy for the first time. The grandmother eventually devises a way of gaining control over her granddaughter once again: she pays a young Indian boy to marry Eréndira. Once out of the convent, she returns to her grandmother.

The love-struck Ulises proposes marriage and an escape from the grandmother. He shows her his potential wealth: the oranges that he and his father ship across the border are grown with diamonds inside. The young pair takes Ulises's father's truck and a pistol, and hastily depart for the border. The grandmother presents the military authorities with a letter of recommendation from a politician. The military consequently chase the couple and eventually catch them on the highway.

Eréndira returns to her previous life in the tent in the desert, paying her debt to her grandmother. The latter offers her a vision for life in the future: Eréndira could someday too, like the grandmother, be a person of power and influence. Ulises, however, once again appears to save her. Eréndira does not hesitate in asking him if he is capable of killing their dominator. He promises to do so, but it proves to be an almost impossible feat. First he attempts to poison her, making a birthday cake with enough arsenic to kill a colony of rats. The only visible effect the venom has on the old woman is her loss of hair. The determined fiancé then places dynamite in the grandmother's piano; the explosion destroys everything but the intended victim. Finally, Ulises stabs the grandmother to death. The old woman dies in a puddle of green blood, an image which recalls the romances of chivalry.

Except for this scene at the end, it is an entertaining story with touches of magic and even an optimistic tone at the conclusion. The magic always occurs in a positive context. For example, after Ulises falls in love, the jar he touches turns colors. The magic of the diamond-filled oranges seems to offer a future for the pair of lovers. Sometimes Eréndira and Ulises communicate with a magical type of telepathy. In the end, the magic of love dominates over the combined forces of evil.

The paradigm of exploitation is clearly delineated, with the grandmother, the military, and the government representing the exploiters. In addition to the direct collaboration the grandmother receives from the military and a senator, it is notable that the primary users of Eréndira's sexual services are soldiers. Eréndira, of course, functions as the exploited subject. The purchaser of her virginity, in fact, deals with her strictly as an object: "He considered the strength of her thighs, the size of her breasts, the diameter of her hips. He didn't say a word until he had some calculation of what she was worth."[9]

The reader's skepticism concerning the act of interpretation is reinforced from the story's first anecdote. It is the grandmother's act of interpretation of the series of unfortunate events concerning the candelabra that ruins the girl's life. The grandmother's total power, however, makes her interpretation the only one, and one that is never questioned. Eréndira not only does not interpret, but rarely even speaks. The power of the word is limited to the grandmother. One of Eréndira's few affirmations is in the convent, when she states "soy feliz" ("I am happy").

A playful communication between author and reader takes place at the beginning of the sixth section of the story. Just after the fleeing lovers have been apprehended at the end of the previous section, the narrator intervenes at the beginning of the sixth section to relate his own personal relationship with the protagonist. He states in first person: "Las conocí en esa época . . . ." ("It was around that time that I came to know them. . . ," (43). The intervention of the narrator at this tense moment of the story is a playful reminder of the work's fictionality. The Latin American reader will also recognize a reference at this point to Rafael Escalona, a famous Colombian musician. Readers of García Márquez understand that the mention of Alvaro Cepeda Samudio is an inside joke with a writer and one of García Márquez's best friends. The initial pages of this section also recall the previous stories, with allusions to the spider from the first story in the volume, Blacaman the Good, and others. In addition to providing a sense of wholeness to the volume and completing a pattern for the reader, the presence of these characters is a reminder of the fictionality of the work for the literal interpreter of texts. The reader fictionalized in the text thus enjoys superiority over the ingenuous character of this fictional Guajira.

García Márquez's interest in power as fictionalized in this story points to a direction of his fiction of the 1970s and the one novel of the decade. *The Autumn of the Patriarch* will deal with power. Before its publication, García Márquez begins to change some characteristics of his style. The story "The Last Voyage of the Ghost Ship" is a notable step in this process. Like the title story, it deals with power.

"The Last Voyage of the Ghost Ship" is a story told by an omniscient narrator in some ways similar to the narrator of *The Autumn of the Patriarch*. An omniscient narrator outside the story is in control, but he cedes the story to other speakers without any punctuation indicators of the change. These changes of speaker all take place in a one-paragraph and one-sentence story of nine pages in the original Spanish edition.

The first two lines of this one-sentence story are as follows: "Now they're going to see who I am, he said to himself in his strong new man's voice. . . ."[10] The initial part of the phrase is the first of numerous admonitions the boy-protagonist will deliver relating to the power he will exercise in the future. The verb in the original Spanish, "van a ver" ("you will see" or "they will see") is ambiguous in Spanish: it could be directed to the readership to whom the story is directed ("*ustedes* van a ver") or it could refer to a group of characters within the story ("*ellos* van a ver"). It soon becomes evident that the verb refers to "they," but the ambiguity of the initial lines both involves the reader and poses the question of what this character will prove with such determination. The combination of the provocative announcement and the description of the voice make his affirmation questionable. "Why does this person insist so much?" the reader may ask.

The protagonist's motives and personality are never totally clarified, but a review of his words and actions can provide room for some speculation. His obsession is a transatlantic ship which he claims to have seen near this port city. No one either believes him or takes him seriously. The first time he sees it he is a child. Because of his own uncertainties, he tells no one of what he has seen. A year later the ship reappears, and this time the boy tells his mother of the incredible vessel. This mother claims he is losing his mind from so much night life. When he takes his mother to actually see the ship for herself the following year, she dies.

The story culminates in his successful encounter with the ship. His frustrated attempts at any communication with the townspeople about it aid the reader in understanding his determination and even obsession. He repeats the phrase of the story's first line, "now they're going to see who I am," as he rows into the bay to meet the boat.

Then he guides the enormous ship with his lantern so that it finally crashes ashore. The unbelievers of the town have in their presence a spectacle seven times the size of the entire town.

If this story affirms anything, it is a celebration and exaltation of the imagination. What seemed to have been the product of a child's imagination, left unrecognized, eventually becomes an overwhelming presence in the town, undeniable for all. The child's successful beaching of the fantastic boat affirms the value of the individual's imagination.

The intercalation of the voice of the protagonist within the standard omniscient narration creates several effects. It produces a well-defined dichotomy between the outside world of the omniscient narrator—the world of the town—and the protagonist—his psychological makeup. The townspeople are uniformly disbelievers of the protagonist's story concerning the ship. After his second sighting of it he tells his mother, who is the first speaker in the text after the protagonist: "because your brain's rotting away from doing so many things backward, sleeping during the day and going out at night like a criminal . . ." (189). The protagonist suffers both this humiliation from his mother and the general opprobrium of the town as the son of a family in disgrace. The mother's mysterious death worsens his situation among the townspeople. The humble social role he occupies in the town perhaps helps explain his secret urge for recognition and power. He repeats the story's initial phrase throughout the narration: "now they're going to see who I am." The desire for power becomes an obsession by the time the boat appears for the last time. At this point the narrator first describes him "babeando de rabia," followed by the affirmation once again that "now they're going to see who I am." In the following phrase the narrator reiterates the protagonist's secret determination to carry out his plan, and the obsessed boy rows out into the bay, repeating still another time "now they're going to see who I am." The constant movement between exterior and interior views of the story's events makes this the most interesting psychological portrayal in the volume.

The use of one sentence for the entire story makes it a technical tour de force for both García Márquez and the protagonist. Both author and protagonist carry the reader to the dual denouement that is the simultaneous culmination of obsessive movement: for the reader this culmination is the landing of the ship and the discovery of the long-awaited but naturally anticipated period after the story's last word. The use of one sentence also has the effect of suggesting the unity of the boy's obsession.[11] As an obsessive act and for the sake of unity, the use of one sentence is an effective synthesis of theme and technique for the reader.

The protagonist in this story seems to seek power for the sake of power, but it is an abstract notion never explained. "Death Constant Beyond Love" also deals with power, but it is clearly political power. It is a story about a corrupt forty-two-year-old politician who faces death within six months. He is Senator Onésimo Sánchez, who visits a small town during his campaign for reelection. The story tells of his political maneuvers and newfound love for one of the town's inhabitants, Laura Farina.

The story begins with Senator Sánchez's arrival at the town, Rosal del Virrey. The isolated desert town lives off the contraband that ships bring at night. Senator Onésimo Sánchez witnesses the masses who attend his public ceremony—the Indians trucked into the town and paid to attend the speech. Despite his profound concern over the doctor's admonition about his death, he performs his political ritual and repeats, once again, his well-memorized speech. The remainder of the political act is an exercise in the manipulation of appearances: during his speech his helpers throw paper animals in the air; others place artificial trees around the back of the multitude; a facade of cardboard houses painted with red bricks and glass windows covers the miserable houses behind it in which the people live. The farce ends with his promises for everything from rain machines to special oils that will make vegetables grow.

The senator had known the Farina family since the days of his first political campaign, when Nelson Farina had asked the politician for his influence in acquiring false papers. Onésimo Sánchez kindly refused the request. Nelson is the father of the beautiful Laura Farina. For this trip the senator makes to the town, the father dresses Laura in her best clothes and sends her to the residence the senator has rented in the town. She is told to wait for the politician while he entertains the local oligarchy in the next room. He explains to them that his reelection is good business for them as well as for him, since he wins his votes because of the region's poverty, and the local elite lives off the poor.

After this meeting, Laura is allowed to visit the senator. The senator immediately understands that her father has sent her as a lover. The politician's amorous intentions are temporarily inhibited when he discovers that she is wearing a chastity belt her father will unlock only after the senator has complied with the previously requested political favor.

The senator lives in the terrible solitude of power and the lack of love, as is evident in the story's ending. He tells Laura to stay rather than get her father's key because "It is good to be with someone when one is alone." She cradles him in her arms as a child where he succumbs to a "terror" which is not explained. The reader can assume it is the terror of solitude and death. Six months and eleven days later he dies in that very position in her arms.

"Death Constant Beyond Love" is a story about different facets of political power. García Márquez ridicules the machinations of politics as practiced in many Western democracies by exaggerating, perhaps only slightly, their capacity for corruption. The characterization of the despot who lives in the solitude of power and desperate for an authentic human relationship—such as love—will be fully elaborated in *The Autumn of the Patriarch.*

The stories from this period represent a transition from the Macondo fiction to what will eventually become the novel about a dictator. They offer a series of paradigms of exploitation, from the children exploited in "Blacaman" and "Innocent Eréndira" to the financial exploitation of the poor old winged man in the first story. García Márquez's ability to entertain with a humor ranging from subtle understatement to wild and irrational invention is present throughout. As entertainments and even children's stories, they do not lend themselves to the type of broad-sweeping interpretations that the Macondo fiction—especially *One Hundred Years of Solitude*—seemed to demand. The themes and techniques explored in this volume—from the sentence structure to the nature of power—will lead to another book of more ambitious and epic proportions than these stories, namely, *The Autumn of the Patriarch.*

Chapter Six
The Autumn of
the Patriarch (1975)

Introduction and Plot

The publication of this novel about a dictator disappointed some of those readers who had associated García Márquez exclusively with the enchantment and accessibility of Macondo. It does not take place in Macondo and is more difficult to read than any of García Márquez's other novels. Judged strictly on its own instrinsic artistic merit, however, *The Autumn of the Patriarch* is a major book for both García Márquez and the field of the contemporary Latin-American novel. It was one of several Latin-American novels appearing in the 1970s dealing with a dictator.

The novel of the dictator is a venerable tradition in Latin America. The two best known initial novels of this type were *Tirando Banderas* (1926) by the Spaniard Ramón del Valle Inclán and *El señor presidente* (1946) by Miguel Angel Asturias. The decade of the 1970s saw the startling empowerment of military dictatorships in Latin America, particularly in the Southern Cone. As if by tacit agreement, major novelists, such as Alejo Carpentier, Augusto Roa Bastos, and García Márquez all published novels on dictators: Carpentier's *Reasons of State* appeared in 1974 and Roa Bastos's *Yo el Supremo (I, the supreme)* in the following year. García Márquez had begun his project at the end of a dictatorship that preceded these sanguine *caudillos* of the 1970s, that of Pérez Jiménez, ruler of Venezuela during the 1950s. Upon arriving in Caracas from Europe in 1958, García Márquez witnessed the downfall of Pérez Jiménez and the concurrent spectacle created by the outburst of a national celebration in Venezuela. The figure of Pérez Jiménez, nevertheless, was just a point of departure. García Márquez began reading histories of dictators, books containing historical anecdotes that can make the most fantastic Latin-American fiction read like stodgy realism. For example, García Márquez has told of reading about a recent Haitian dictator, Duvalier, who ordered all black dogs in the country killed because he believed one of his political enemies had transformed himself into a black dog; Maximiliano Hernández Martínez of El Salvador invented a pendulum to weigh his food before eating to assure it was not poisoned.[1] *The Autumn of the Patriarch* contains anecdotes from these history books. The author explains:

My intention was always to make a synthesis of all the Latin American dictators, but especially those from the Caribbean. Nevertheless, the personality of Juan Vicente Gómez [of Venezuela] was so strong, in addition to the fact that he exercised a special fascination over me, that undoubtedly the Patriarch has much more of him than anyone else. In any case, the mental image that I have of both is the same. Which doesn't mean, of course, that he is the same character as the one in the book, but rather an idealization of his image.[2]

The protagonist of this novel, of course, is a dictator. A more precise definition of the theme, however, is not dictatorships but power. From those days of Pérez Jiménez's fall García Márquez was intrigued by the "mystery of power," as he called it.[3] He had dealt with this abstract notion in such stories as "Big Mama's Funeral" and several stories written between 1968 and 1972 (see chapter 5). The project on the theme of power was begun in the late 1950s, set aside, and then completed after *One Hundred Years of Solitude*. The result was a stunning and enormously complex performance in the craft of fiction.

One indicator of the change in García Márquez's fiction is the fact that this novel is not located in Colombia. The exact location of the dictator's realm is impossible to establish, although it is a nation in the Caribbean area. Some readers will find themselves locating the imaginary country in Venezuela, while others will envision an island. The text's ambiguities make both possibilities plausible. The problem is that there are references to locations that different readers will associate with specific areas of the Caribbean. García Márquez, who knows all the Caribbean intimately, explains the novel's locale as follows:

Undoubtedly, it is a country in the Caribbean. But it is a Caribbean mixed with the Spanish Caribbean and the English Caribbean. You are aware that I know the Caribbean island by island, city by city. And I've put everything there. What is mine first. The bordello where I lived in Barranquilla, the Cartagena of my student days, the little port bars where I used to eat when leaving the newspaper at four in the morning, and even the ships that at dawn would leave for Aruba and Curazao filled with whores. In it there are streets that are like the Calle del Comercio in Panamá, street corners of the old section of Havana, of San Juan and of Guajira. But also places that belong to the English Antilles, with their Hindus, Chinese, and Dutch.[4]

To speak of a plot is an equally ambiguous proposition, since there is no plot developed in a consistent fashion. The novel involves a series of anecdotes which relate to the life of a dictator identified as the General. The anecdotes do not appear in chronological order; in addition, they sometimes include such gross anachronisms as the presence of Christopher Columbus and American marines in the same scene.

The first chapter begins with the discovery of the General's rotting corpse in the presidential palace. The narrative moves quickly to anecdotes during his lifetime. The central anecdote in this chapter is what is identified as his "first death": his government-appointed double, Patricio Aragonés, dies. The General is able to observe the spectacle of popular celebration over his death. He learns a valuable lesson about the fragility of power, and consequently has those who had taken over his government assassinated, while he rewards those who mourned his death. At the end of the chapter he looks out the window facing the sea of his palace, and he sees that the marines have abandoned the dock and three Spanish ships are arriving.

The action of the second chapter is centered on the woman with whom the General falls obsessively in love, Manuela Sánchez. She is characterized somewhat like Laura Farina in "Death Constant Beyond Love." Manuela, of working-class origins, has a stunning beauty which overwhelms the General, who is rendered helpless at her sight. The relationship between Senator Onésimo Sánchez and Laura Farina is also quite similar to the one between the General and Manuela Sánchez: both men are impotent and childlike figures; both women are more mother figures for these two men than potential lovers. Manuela Sánchez disappears at the end of the chapter, never to be found, despite the rumors of her having been sighted in different parts of the Caribbean, from Aracataca to Panamá. The General realizes he is condemned to dying without her love, and envisions a death lying facedown between the ages of 107 and 232 years.

The third chapter deals with the politics of power. His power seems limitless, as he is capable of arranging the weather, and signaling with his finger so that trees give fruit, animals grow, and men prosper. A revealing scene with respect to the General's politics occurs when an idealistic young foreigner visits the General to request support. The young man needs logistic and political support for the conservative cause, for which he professes his willingness to die. Hearing these words, the General recommends that the young idealist not be a fool, for he should enjoy the country while he is alive. The patriarch does not aid this conservative idealist. One of the novel's most memorable scenes occurs at the end of the chapter when the General intuits a plot against his government. He decides the culprit is one of his most intimate friends, General Rodrigo de Aguilar. The guests wait an inordinate amount of time for Rodrigo de Aguilar's arrival, but he does finally arrive at the banquet. The chapter ends with his grand entrance:

and then the curtains parted and the distinguished Major General Rodrigo de Aguilar entered on a silver tray stretched out full length on a garnish of cauliflower and laurel leaves, steeped with spices, oven brown, embellished with the uniform of five golden almonds for solemn occasions and the limitless loops for valor on the sleeve of his right arm, fourteen pounds of medals on his chest and a sprig of parsley in his mouth, ready to be served at a banquet of comrades by the official carvers to the petrified horror of the guests as without breathing we witness the exquisite ceremony of carving and serving, and when every plate held an equal portion of minister of defense stuffed with pine nuts and aromatic herbs, he gave the order to begin, eat hearty gentlemen.[5]

The General's power begins to wane in the fourth chapter. His ability to understand either his loss of power or a diminishing contact with reality seems limited. His aging mother, Bendición Alvarado, becomes the object of an obsession on the part of the General to have her canonized. The result of his campaign is her being given the status of "civil sanctity" and being named patroness of the nation. Near the end of the chapter he initiates an intimate relationship with his future wife, Nazareno Leticia. The General becomes so terrorized by the prospect of physical intimacy with her, however, that he defecates in his shorts.

The last two chapters narrate his final demise. The General marries Nazareno Leticia and has a child by her. The wife and child are assassinated and dogs rip apart their corpses in a public plaza. The General hires a smooth and handsome henchman, Saenz de la Barra, to carry out the sadistic assassinations of the government needs. The supreme dictator celebrates his one hundredth anniversary in power, but thereafter his reign is one of decadence in all senses of the word. He dies unsure of the possession of the power that he exercised and by which he was tormented in the solitude of his dictatorship.

Structure, Theme, and Narrative Technique

This basic anecdote as described above could be reduced to a nuclear verb: "A corpse is found."[6] This simple anecdote is the point of departure and frame for the actual storytelling. Each chapter begins with this basic anecdote, describing the discovery of the General's corpse in the presidential palace. The total narrative content of the novel, however, is developed beyond this discovery: it relates the General's entire life by transforming this basic anecdote of the framework into a more complete biographical revelation.

The transformation of this anecdotal material to the actual story of the text can be described by considering the novel's six chapters as a system of progressive apertures.[7] That is, the first chapter is developed on the basis of an aperture, the second on another aperture, and so on. The qualifier "progressive" underlines the fact that the apertures occur at an earlier point in each of the six chapters. These apertures occur in each of the six chapters on four levels. It must be noted, however, that each level will be discussed separately only for the clarity of analysis. In the novel's experience these levels occur simultaneously. The four levels of aperture are (1) the opening or the original situation, (2) the opening of the sentence length, (3) the opening of narrative focus, and (4) the opening of a "seen" reality. The structure of progressive apertures provides for a dynamic experience.

The first chapter establishes the basic circumstances involved with the discovery of the General's corpse, the original situation (first level) in the presidential palace. In this first scene an unidentified narrator within the story describes some vultures entering the presidential palace. With this sign, the narrator notes, he and some of his accomplices dare to enter the premises. Upon their entrance, the narrative describes the physical surroundings—for the most part decaying objects in the palace. After an initial two-and-one-half-page description of the physical surroundings, this narrator provides the first description of the General's body, an image that recurs throughout the novel: "y allí lo vimos a él con el uniforme de lienzo sin insignias, las polainas, la espuela de oro en el talón izquierdo, más viejo que todos los hombres y todos los animales viejos de la tierra y del agua, y estaba tirado en el suelo, bocabajo, con el brazo derecho doblado bajo la cabeza para que le sirviera de almohada, como había dormido noche tras noche durante todas las noches de su larguísima vida de déspota solitario"[8] ("and there we saw him, in his denim uniform without insignia, boots, the gold spur on his left heel, older than all old men and all old animals on land or sea, and he was stretched out on the floor, face down, his right arm bent under his head as a pillow, as he had slept night after night every night of his ever so long life of a solitary despot," 9–10). At approximately this point the narration changes from exclusively a description of the immediate surroundings to the telling of the General's story: "Sólo cuando lo volteamos para verle la cara comprendimos que era imposible reconocerlo aunque no hubiera estado carcomido de gallinazos, porque ninguno de nosotros lo había visto nunca . . ." (8) ("Only when we turned him over to look at his face did we realize that it was impossible to recognize him, even though his face had not been pecked away by vultures, because none of us had ever seen him. . . ," 10).

By noting that none of them had ever actually seen the General before his death, the narrator has changed from a description of the physical surroundings to relating *past* circumstances. This is the point in the first chapter that may be identified as the "aperture" in the narrative—an opening of the original situation into a broader story.

Each of the five remaining chapters establishes the original situation as described above and follows it with an aperture to narration of the General's past. In the second chapter the narrator begins to integrate the elements of the General's story almost immediately upon beginning the description of the original situation in the presidential palace. The first sentence of the second chapter reads as follows: "La segunda vez que lo encontraron carcomido por los gallinazos en la misma oficina, con la misma ropa y en la misma posición, ninguno de nosotros era bastante viejo para recordar lo que ocurrió la primera vez, pues siempre había otra verdad detrás de la verdad" (46) ("The second time he was found, chewed away by vultures in the same office, wearing the same clothes and in the same position, none of us was old enough to remember what had happened the first time, but we knew that no evidence of his death was final, because there was always another truth behind the truth," 45). The sentence may be divided into three parts that demonstrate the way the structure of the novel functions. The first part, to the word "posición," refers to the original situation, the corpse. The second part, from "ninguno" to "primera vez," refers to that part of the story already learned by the reader, in addition to the original situation. In the third part, the story opens to present new information—that is, information other than the original situation and what the reader has already learned. By the second page of this chapter, however, the narrator has returned to the original situation, employing a short sentence that makes reference to it: "Tampoco el escrutinio meticuloso de la casa aportó elemento válido para establecer su identidad" (48) ("Nor did the meticulous scrutiny of the house bring forth any valid element to establish his identity," 46). (It is important to note the use of short sentences at the beginning of the chapters and also for reference to the original situation.) Then the narrator describes more of the physical surroundings—Bendición Alvarado's room. After approximately two and a half pages the complete opening can be identified, changing the focus from the original situation to telling the General's story: "Al contrario de la ropa, las descripciones de sus historiadores le quedaban grandes . . ." (50) ("Contrary to what his clothing showed, the descriptions made by his historians made him very big. . . ," 47). From this point in the chapter there is no more description of the physical surroundings, and the narrative opens exclusively to the narration of the General's story. By the third chapter the transformation from the revelation of details concerning the original situation to reference to the known story occurs earlier, and the original situation is less important than in the two previous chapters (again, stressing the "progressive" nature of the structure).

The first sentence refers to the cadaver: "Así lo encontraron en las vísperas de su otoño, cuando el cadáver era en realidad el de Patricio Aragonés, y así volvimos a encontrarlo muchos años más tarde en una época de tantas incertidumbres que nadie podía rendirse a la evidencia de que fuera suyo aquel cuerpo senil carcomido de gallinazos y plagado de parásitos de fondo de mar" (89) ("That was how they found him on the evening of his autumn, when the corpse was really that of Patricio Aragonés, and that was how we found him again many years later during a moment of such uncertainty that no one could give in to the evidence that the senile body there gouged by vultures and infested with parasites from the depths of the sea was his," 83). In this sentence there is one reference with a scope beyond the original situation: "during a moment of such uncertainty." The second sentence refers to the physical (his hand), and from this point the sentence moves toward the past. By the third sentence (still on the first page of the chapter), there are no references to the immediate physical surroundings. and the chapter has opened up to narration of the General's story. The fourth sentence (first and second page, in Spanish) and the fifth sentence (second, third, and fourth pages) make no reference to the physical environment, and mention the corpse only as a point of departure for relating to the story beyond this situation. These two sentences can be identified as the point of definitive opening of the chapter from the original situation to narration of the General's story. There are no more references to the original situation, and the opening has occurred on the second page of the chapter. The original situation has now become less important, being used more as a technical point of departure.

The first sentence of the fourth chapter deals with the General's story, making no reference to the original situation. The second sentence does refer to the corpse, and then continues beyond this original situation to relate popular opinion concerning the General: "Sin embargo, mientras se adelantaban los trámites para componer y embalsamar el cuerpo, hasta los menos cándidos esperábamos sin confesarlo el cumplimiento de predicciones antiguas, como que el día de su muerte el lodo de los cenegales había de regresar por sus afluentes hasta las cabaceras, que había de llover sangre . . ." (129) ("Yet, while the plans for reassembling and embalming the body went forward, even the most candid among us waited without so confessing for the fulfillment of ancient predictions, such as the one that said that on the day of his death the mud from the swamps would go back upriver to its source, that it would rain blood. . . ," 120). The third sentence makes no reference to the General's physical environment. It continues relating the rumors and versions about his life. At this point on the first page the opening to narration of the General's past takes place.

In the fifth chapter the first sentence refers specifically to the original situation: "Poco antes del anochecer, cuando acabamos de sacar los cascarones podridos de las vacas y pusimos un poco de arreglo en aquel desorden de fábula, aún no habíamos conseguido que el cadáver se pareciera a la imagen de su leyenda" (169) ("Shortly before nightfall, when we finished taking out the rotten husks of the cows and putting a little order into that fabulous disarray, we were still unable to tell if the corpse looked like its legendary image," 157). The second sentence also refers to this original situation; the narrator explains the attempts made to prepare the Generals' corpse. The third sentence functions as a bridge between relating the original situation and opening to the past. It remains within the framework of the original situation, but extends the immediate present (the specificity of the corpse) by relating the meeting of officials in a nearby room ("salón de consejo") in which they begin to decide upon the division of power: "Mientras tanto, en el salón de consejo de gobierno invocábamos la unión de todos contra el despotismo de siglos para repartirse por partes iguales el botín de su poder, pues todos . . ." (169) ("In the cabinet room meanwhile we called for the unity of all against the despotism of centuries so we could divide up the booty of his power in equal parts, because everyone. . . ," 157). The "salón de consejo" is not precisely within the scope of the original situation, and thus serves as a physical link between this situation and the relating of the General's story. The fourth sentence creates the actual opening of this narrative: "Nos encontrábamos inermes ante esa evidencia, comprometidos con un cuerpo pestilente que no éramos capaces de sustituir en el mundo porque él se había negado en sus instancias seniles a tomar ninguna determinación sobre el destino de la patria después de él, había resistido con una terquedad de viejo a cuantas sugerencias se le hicieron desde que el gobierno . . ." (170) ("We were defenseless against that evidence, compromised by a pestilential corpse that we were incapable of replacing in the world because he had refused in his senile insistence to take any decision concerning the destiny of the nation after he was gone, with the invincible stubborness of an old man he had resisted all suggestions made to him ever since the government. . . ," 158). At the begining of the sentence the narrator makes note of the "pestilential corpse." Then, however, the sentence begins to describe the General's actions (having refused to make any provisions for what was to be arranged after his death) previous to this basic situation, and thus marks the point of opening in the narrative: the chapter continues as the story of the General and there are no more references to the original situation.

In the last chapter, the sixth, the aperture occurs on the first page. Several parts of the sentence refer to the original situation: "Ahí estaba, pues, como si hubiera sido él aunque no lo fuera, acostado en la mesa de banquetes . . ."; "más temible muerto que vivo con el guante de raso relleno sobre el pecho . . ." (214) ("There he was, then, as if it had been he even though it might not be, lying on the banquet table . . ."; "more fearsome dead than alive, the velvet glove stuffed with cotton on a chest. . . ," 203). Toward the end of the first page the narrator changes the focus to a previous discussion, which, in turn, leads to opening the narrative to related matters: "discutíamos palabra por palabra el boletín final con la noticia que nadie se atrevía . . ." (219) ("we were discussing the final bulletin with the news that no one dared believe word by word. . . ," 203).

Both tradition and innovation are descriptive of the effect of this aperture on the first level, or the original situation. The manner in which physical space functions in this novel corresponds in a sense to the realist-naturalist tradition: the beginning of the novel focuses more precisely on the physical space; then, after the physical environment has been described at the outset of the novel, the narrator elaborates the anecdotal material with less background provided for the reader in terms of setting. On the other hand, the reader does not experience place in exactly the same manner as in the traditional novel. García Márquez manipulates physical space to such a degree that the reader finds himself progressively more limited in terms of physical space and background setting, and at the same time progressively more involved in the elaboration of the General's life.

These apertures that function as points indicating change from the original situation to the General's story are supported technically by the use of a progressive opening of the length of the sentence.[9] This is the second level of aperture. The sentences lengthen at approximately the same point in each of the chapters as the noted point at which the transformation from the original situation to the General's story occurs. In each chapter the beginning sentences might be identified as a normal length. The sentences then expand in length as the chapter continues. The progressive nature of this development is evidenced by the fact that each chapter has fewer sentences: chapter 1 has thirty-one sentences; chapter 2, twenty-four sentences; chapter 3, nineteen sentences; chapter 4, eighteen sentences; chapter 5, fifteen sentences; and chapter 6 is a single sentence.

In the first chapter the sentences on the first page might be described as a "normal" length—that is, of eight, eight, and five lines, respectively, in the text. The fourth sentence (ending the first page and beginning the second) expands to twenty-one lines. Throughout the next seven pages (to page 12, in the Spanish text) the length of the sentences varies, but remains approximately within the limits of the sentences on the first two pages, ranging from a few lines in length to a full page (thirty-five lines in the text). Then, on page 12, the first significant opening of the length of the sentence takes place, with the sentence on pages 12 and 13 being sixty-four lines in length. From this point, sentences become progressively longer, or at least tend to maintain the length of the longer sentences observed (about a page or slightly more).

The change in sentence length is abrupt in the second chapter. On the first two pages the sentences tend to be relatively short. As in the first chapter, the first sentence is eight lines. The second sentence, the longest in the beginning pages, consists of thirty lines (slightly less than a page); the remainder of the sentences on the first two pages range from three to twenty-one lines. At approximately the same point where the narrative changes its focus from the original situation to the General's story, the sentence length expands to a page or more. The change from the original situation to past description has been noted on page 50 in this second chapter (in Spanish text). The initial expansion of the sentence also takes place on page 50; the sentence on pages 50–51 is thirty-five lines, or a full page, in length. From this point the narrative opens (both in its circumstance and in sentence length), and the remaining sentences of the chapter tend to be longer than a page rather than shorter than a page.

The progressive nature of the openings in sentence length is equally evident in the third, fourth, and fifth chapters. In the third chapter there are three sentences before the extension of the length, and the fourth and fifth chapters contain two sentences and one sentence of normal length, respectively. The sentences that mark these openings in the three chapters are of twenty-eight lines, forty-nine lines, and twenty-two lines. In each case the change in sentence length is noted at the same place in the text that marked the change from the original situation as discussed.

The last chapter begins "Ahí estaba, pues como si hubiera . . ." (219) ("There he was, then, as if it had been. . . , 203). This is a reference to the corpse and the immediate situation. Within this same sentence the chapter opens to related matters on the first page ("we were discussing"). The opening in terms of sentence length reaches the extreme; the entire chapter is one sentence of one thousand eight hundred and twenty-five lines (in Spanish text). This change is in accordance with the progressive nature of the structure as it has been discussed. Although more extreme than in the previous chapters, this length is a logical step in the development: sentences have become progressively longer in each chapter.

The progressive and precise manner of organizing the sentence length in correspondence with the opening of the original situation contributes to the formation of the narrative system García Márquez constructs in this novel. Although apparently lacking in punctuation (in the first reading), this novel employs punctuation in a manner different from its traditional function in prose; the specific placement of the period corresponds to the poetic use of textual space. Such technical precision supports García Márquez's contention that this novel is a "poem about the solitude of power."[10]

The third level of aperture, also corresponding to the first two, is the opening of narrative focus. The narrative focus in which each chapter begins is relatively limited; then it opens to other points of view, and in some cases to multiple points of view within the same sentence. This variation of the narrative's focus, by use of the apertures to be described, has various effects and is a particularly important aspect of the experience of the novel.[11]

An unidentified narrator within the story recounts the beginning pages of the first chapter. He and other unidentified accomplices enter the presidential palace to discover the rotting corpse. For this reason this narrator will be referred to as the "narrator-discoverer." Thus, the initial pages are narrated in the first-person plural ("we saw"). The first sentence does not identify a narrator as necessarily within the story, and technically it could be told by a narrator outside the story: "Durante el fin de semana los gallinazos se metieron por los balcones de la casa presidencial, destrozaron a picotazos las mallas de alambre de las ventanas y removieron con sus alas el tiempo estancado en el interior, y en la madrugada del lunes la ciudad despertó de su letargo de siglos con una tibia y tierna brisa de muerto grande y de podrida grandeza." (5) ("Over the weekend the vultures got into the presidential palace by pecking through the screens on the balcony windows and the flapping of their wings stirred up the stagnant time inside, and at dawn on Monday the city awoke out of its lethargy of centuries with the warm, soft breeze of a great man dead and rotting grandeur," 7).

From the beginning of the next sentence the position of the narrator within the story is evident: "Sólo entonces nos atrevimos a entrar . . ." (5) ("Only then did we dare go in. . . ," 7). For approximately the next three pages the narrative remains within the scope of this narrator who enters the palace in the company of others. By the fourth page, however, the narrative begins to open to other speakers. The first change occurs on page 9 in the Spanish text (page 11 in English text) in which the narrator inside the story is relating details about the physical environment, and suddenly the narrative changes to several words that originate from another speaker: "y una tarde de enero habíamos visto una vaca contemplando el crepúsculo desde el balcón presidencial, imagínese, una vaca en el balcón de la patria, qué cosa más inicua, qué país de mierda" (9) ("and one January afternoon we had seen a cow contemplating the sunset from the presidential balcony, just imagine, a cow on the balcony of the nation, what an awful thing, what a shitty country," 11). The "just imagine" interrupts the original narrator's account through the use of this conversational style. In this case the narrative has changed from pure narration to inferring a live dialogue. This point in the narrative, noted as the opening of the narrative focus (transcending the limits of the narrator-discoverer), occurs in the same sentence already discussed, changing from the original situation to the story of the General. Later in the chapter, as the sentences lengthen, the length of the communications by other speakers is extended.

The second chapter begins once more with the relatively "closed" narrative focus of the narrator-discoverer. The first change in this focus, an expansion beyond the limits of this narrator, occurs in the place identified as the point of aperture on the two other levels, on the fourth and fifth pages of the chapter (page 50–51; pages 47–48 in English text). Here, the narrator changes his scope from a general knowledge to the specific words of the General. The key sentence in which this change takes place reads as follows: (I quote

it through the first change in narrative focus): "Esta certidumbre
parecía válida inclusive para él, pues se sabía que era un hombre sin
padre como los déspotas más ilustres de la historia, que el único
pariente que se le conoció y tal vez único que tuvo fue su madre de
mi alma Bendición Alvarado a quien los textos escolares . . ." (51)
("That certainly seemed valid even for him, as he knew that he was
a man without a father like the most illustrious despots of history,
that the only relative known to him and perhaps the only one he
had was his mother of my heart Bendición Alvarado to whom the
school texts. . . ," 48) The words "se sabía" ("it was known")
exemplify the level of communication identified as general knowledge—that which everybody (or all the inhabitants) knows.[12] Later
in this sentence the first opening beyond the limits of this narrator
and general knowledge is noted with the word "mi," either the
actual speech of the General or the narrator's imitation of his words.
Three additional parts of this sentence express a focus beyond general
knowledge. First, the narrator states: "a quien él proclamó por
decreto matriarca de la patria con el argumento simple de que madre
no hay sino una, la mía, una rara mujer de origen incierto . . ."
(51) ("and whom he proclaimed matriarch of the land by decree
with the simple argument that there is no mother but one, mine,
a strange woman of uncertain origins. . . ," 48). Later in the same
sentence the first longer opening of narrative focus in the chapter
takes place in the voice of the General's mother:

ni podía soportar que había dicho en una fiesta diplomática que estoy
cansada de rogarle a Dios que tumben a mi hijo, porque esto de vivir en
la casa presidencial es como estar a toda hora con la luz prendida, señor,
y lo había dicho con la misma verdad natural con que un día de la patria
. . . (51)

nor could they bear the fact that at a diplomatic party she had said I'm
tired of begging God to overthrow my son, because all this business of
living in the presidential palace is like having the lights on all the time,
sir, and she had said it with the same naturalness with which on one
national holiday. . . , (49).

At the end of the sentence another phrase changes to the mother's
actual words, and the last two words are of the General. From this
point in the chapter the focus of the narrative has been opened, and

the voices continue to vary as the chapter proceeds, such changes becoming more frequent and lengthy.

In accordance with the progressive nature of the structure, the opening of focus occurs at an earlier point in the third chapter than in the first two. The narrator-discoverer who begins the chapter has entire control of the narrative for only the first page. In the fourth sentence the chapter opens in sentence length and likewise into the past beyond the original situation. It is also this fourth sentence that opens the narrative to speakers other than the narrator-discoverer. This takes place on the second page of the chapter and in the words of Palmerston (page 90 in Spanish; page 84 in English). Palmerston's voice continues for eighteen lines: at this point in the novel the opening of narrative focus not only occurs earlier than in the previous chapters, now there is an *extensive* opening from the beginning of the chapter. The sixth sentence, the longest of the chapter (207 lines in Spanish), contains numerous changes in speaker.

The fourth chapter is structured quite similarly to the third, contains approximately the same number of sentences, and does not vary significantly from the procedures noted in the third chapter. The chapter opens, in sentence length, in the third sentence (forty-nine lines, in Spanish). With the fourth sentence, of forty lines, the focus expands with the use of short phrases in the voices of characters other than the narrator-discoverer. Thus, on the third page of the chapter (page 131; page 122 in English) a character says "adiós" to the General, and later in the same sentence we find the short phrase: "al pasar con un pañuelo blanco, adiós mi general, adiós, pero él no oía nada desde los lutos crepusculares . . ." (131) ("with a white handkerchief when he passed, hello general sir, hello, but he didn't hear, he had heard nothing since the sunset mourning rites. . . ," 122). From this point, the sentence that opens the narrative focus, the fourth chapter continues with at least short interruptions of the narration of the narrator-discoverer. The opening of the narrative focus takes place slightly earlier in the fifth chapter than in the fourth. The opening to the General's story has been seen in the fourth sentence, and this is the point at which the narrative focus opens beyond the narrator-discoverer. This chapter also contains another of the rare, extensive uninterrupted monologues by the General (thirteen lines on pages 201–2; pages 187–88 in English). It is significant both in theme and structure: (1) the subject of this monologue is his "mar," an object very important to the

General's power, and (2) as in the extensive monologue in the previous chapter, it occurs near the end of the chapter where the length
of the sentence is extended and in the second longest sentence of
the chapter (214 lines).

The last chapter carries the progressive nature of the structure to
its extreme by opening to the General's story on the first page and
extending the sentence to constitute the entire chapter. The use of
various speakers also takes place earlier than before, beginning immediately after the first page of the chapter: "un teniente que iba
de puerta en puerta ordenando cerrar las pocas tiendas que empezaban
a abrirse en la calle del comercio, hoy es feriado nacional gritaba
. . ." (220) ("a lieutenant going from door to door ordering people
to close the doors of the few shops that were beginning to open on
the commercial street, today is a national holiday they shouted,"
204). Other brief changes in the narrative voice follow on the same
page and immediately thereafter. The variety of narrative voices
present in this one-sentence chapter makes it the most complex of
all. These speakers appear more frequently and their communication
is more extensive than in the preceding chapters. At the beginning
of the chapter the first extensive change in narrative focus is communicated in the words of an adolescent girl whom the General
seduces, an act described by her in a monologue of twenty-seven
lines (page 222; page 206 in English). The second monologue on
the following page is by another of his lovers. It also describes the
General's sexual preferences from the point of view of a woman, a
monologue of nineteen lines (page 223; page 207 in English). Afterward and throughout the chapter, there are numerous short dialogues by the General and other characters, such as José Ignacio
Saenz de la Barra, Commander Kitchener, Consul Macdonnal, Bendición Alvarado, Ambassador Kipling, unidentified officials close
to the General, and unidentified citizenry.

One function of the changing narrative focus is to provide a more
complete characterization of the General, which, in turn, is responsible for humorous effects in this characterization. A common
technique is to place emphasis on the General's omnipotence (usually
the "exterior" view of the General) in contrast with his fundamental
simplicity (usually the "interior" view of him). Power is expressed
from the first page as something intangible but perceived by all
under the General's rule. The narrator-discoverer reveals the generalized perception of the General's power by professing to believe

in the General's power to order trees to bear fruit: "power was still not the shoreless bog of the fullness of his autumn but a feverish torrent that we saw gush out of its spring before our very eyes so that all he had to do was point at trees for them to bear fruit and at animals for them to grow and at men for them to prosper . . ." (87). As this passage suggests in both its content and style, according to the "exterior" and distanced view, the General is a God-like figure. [13]

The inside view of the General and his power supports this God-like characterization, and also creates humor by showing the pettiness of his conception of power (in contrast with the grandiosity of the God figure), and his paranoia and puerility. Once the first chapter has opened beyond the generalized view, an omniscient narrator communicates the General's God-like understanding of his capacity to decide "destiny." When he justifies the assassination of officials who betray him, he does so with a God-like expression of being their creator (page 116; page 109 in English).

In contrast with the God-like power that he manipulates both in the view of the citizenry and in his own self-esteem, the inside view consistently emphasizes his pettiness and puerility. Throughout the novel the General carefully and repetitively locks an elaborate combination of "the three crossbars, the three locks, the three bolts" in his room, thus underlining his paranoia. Despite his God-like self-confidence, his friend Rodrigo de Aguilar is the only person "authorized" to defeat him in dominoes. The General's simplicity is an aspect of his characterization not revealed by the narrator-discoverer. The General is characterized as such after the narrative focus has opened to other speakers beyond the voice of the citizenry. In the first chapter, after the narrative opens beyond the narrator-discoverer, an omniscient narrator explains that the General oversees the milking of the cows each day in order to measure the exact amount of milk the presidential carts carry to the city, providing a humorous contrast with the grandiose figure seen by the citizenry, and even with the interior view of himself as a God figure. When the General decides to find his love, Manuela Sánchez, his search for her resembles an adolescent experience: he looks for her in the neighborhood, nervously asks various people for directions to the home he describes, and after introducing himself to her mother, waits anxiously in the living room while her mother knits.

His characterization as a child figure is developed from the beginning of the novel when he is described as a "decrepit child." At one point he joyfully plays with his live siren, wind-up angel, and giant shell. In general, the relationship between the mother and son tends to be a mother-child relationship. For example, she reprimands him about his health and informs him that he must stay home for dinner. After his mother's death, he marries Leticia Nazareno and she assumes the mother role. She teaches him to read and write, the important factor here being the infantile methodology she uses: he recites children's songs.

The technique of contrasting the exterior and interior views of the General is particularly effective in certain passages in which a particular anecdote changes from the exterior to the interior focus within one sentence. For example, an attempted assassination is foiled by the General when, as the potential assassin holds him at gunpoint, he confronts the man and screams: "atrévete cabrón, atrévete" ("I dare you you bastard, I dare you"). When the assassin hesitates, the General attacks him, calls his guards, and orders the victim tortured. After the narration of this anecdote by an omniscient narrator (with occasional interjections by the General), the story is completed by providing at the very end of the sentence the interior focus (of which those who saw him were not aware): "desapareció en la sala de audiencias como un relámpago fugitivo hacia los aposentos privados, entró en el dormitorio, cerró las tres aldabas, los tres pestillos, los tres cerrojos, y se quitó con la punta de los dedos los pantalones que llevaba ensopados de mierda" (123) ("he disappeared into the hearing room like a fugitive lightning flash toward the private quarters, he went into the bedroom, shut the three crossbars, the three bolts, the three locks, and with his fingertips he took off the pants he was wearing that were soaked in shit," 115). Until the narrator reveals the General's reactions in the last three words, the reader's view has been exterior and similar to that of the people observing the General's reactions. The last three words provide the interior contrasting characterization of the General and thus creates the humor.

The fourth, and final, level of aperture in the structure of *The Autumn of the Patriarch* is the opening to a "seen" reality; or one could say that this fourth level is an opening of the dimensions of reality experienced in the novel. Each chapter begins with defined limits of reality—that which can be seen. The reader experiences this manipulation of visible and invisible reality in conjunction with the three other levels of aperture.

In the first scene of the novel, vultures are entering the presidential palace. The first suggestion that the General is dead is thus provided by visual means. From this sentence and throughout the novel, it becomes apparent that only that which is seen may possibly be believed: the General, the citizenry, and the reader learn to believe only what they can see. [14] This problem of visible and invisible reality is fundamental to the main theme of the novel—the General's power—and to the reader's experience. After the description of the vultures, the visible sign of death, the narrator-discoverer emphasizes the importance of what can be *seen:* "y las cosas eran arduamente visibles en la luz decrépita . . ." (5) ("and things were hard to see in the decrepit light," 7). He follows with an elaboration of his realm of the visible, using the verb "to see" repetitively (pages 5–6 in Spanish; pages 7–8 in English). The final use of the verb "to see" at the beginning of the chapter takes place when they discover the General's corpse. Appropriately, upon describing this visible image of the General, the narrative opens to beyond what this narrator can see—the point of aperture in the chapter. In the sentence following the description of the General, for example, the conjugated verbs are "comprender" ("to understand") and "saber" ("to know"). The narrative changes from what can be seen to what is understood, and to what has been related.

The first sentence of the second chapter sets forth the actual theme—the problem of the visible versus illusion—thus discussing the experience of living under the General's power and the process elaborated by the novel's structure: "La segunda vez que lo encontraron carcomido por los gallinazos en la misma oficina, con la misma ropa y en la misma posición, ninguno de nosotros era bastante viejo para recordar lo que ocurrió la primera vez, pero sabíamos que ninguna evidencia de su muerte era terminante, pues siempre había otra verdad detrás de la verdad. Ni siquiera los menos prudentes nos conformábamos con las apariencias . . ." (47) ("The second time he was found, chewed away by vultures in the same office, wearing the same clothes and in the same position, none of us was old enough to remember what had happened the first time, but we knew that no evidence of his death was final, because there was always another truth behind the truth. Not even the least prudent among us would accept. . . ," 45). After this initial suggestion

of one of the novel's fundamental themes, the narrator-discoverer
once more describes the experience of entering the palace by relating
exclusively what he sees: "vimos un sillón de mimbre mordisqueado
por las vacas . . . vimos estuches de pinturas de agua . . . vimos
una tinaja . . ." (48) ("we saw a wicker easy chair nibbled by the
cows . . . we saw watercolor sets . . . we saw a tub. . . ," 46).
When they enter the General's bedroom the verb employed is "to
find" ("encontramos"), rather than "to see," but stress continues to
fall on the tangible. At this point in the chapter the emphasis
changes from what is actually seen to what has been said.

In the third chapter the opening takes place on the first page of
the chapter. The verb "to see" is not employed, but the verb "to
find" functions similarly, indicating something tangible. The narrator-discoverer describes the General in the first sentence of the
chapter: "y así volvimos a encontrarlo muchos años más tarde en
una época de tantas incertidumbres que nadie podía rendirse a la
evidencia de que fuera suyo aquel cuerpo senil carcomido de gallinazos y plagado de parásitos de fondo de mar" (90) ("and that was
how we found him again many years later during a moment of such
uncertainty that no one could give in to the evidence that the senile
body there gouged by vultures and infested with parasites from the
depths of the sea was his," 83). The second sentence also describes
the strictly visible. The next sentence changes the emphasis from
the visible: the narrator explains what it *seemed* like and what they
doubted.

The first sentence of the fifth chapter refers to the problem of the
visible versus the invisible General, the latter being the one that
has been imagined, the one that has been created through general
knowledge, that is, "se dice" ("it is said") or "se contaba" ("it was
told"): "we were still unable to tell if the corpse looked like its
legendary image" (157). In this instance the narrator-discoverer is
in the presence of the visible General, but an attempt is being made
to change him so that he might correspond to the reality—his
legend—that has superseded the real and tangible. The second
sentence involves the actual physical process through which rec-
onciliation of these two realities is attempted. The theme of the
visible versus the invisible reality is abandoned by the third sentence
and the chapter opens beyond this problem to a meeting of officials
after the General's death.

Just as in the previous chapters, the last chapter uses as its point of departure the theme of the visible General versus the popular legend. The first words of the first line emphasize his visual image: "Ahí estaba, pues como si hubiera sido él aunque no lo fuera . . ." (203) ("There he was, then, as if it had been even though. . . ," 203). At this point the theme of the visible versus the invisible has become problematical: it appears to be the General even if it is not, and it is impossible to make any definitive statement concerning the matter. Later in the first page there is another direct reference to the problem of the visible General versus the invisible, in this case affirming the importance of the visible within this fictional world. By the last chapter the characterization of the General only affirms the observation made concerning the reiteration of the verb "to see" in the beginning chapters of the novel: only the visible offers the possibility of being believable, although it certainly does not assure credibility.

This fourth level of the structure is fundamental to the novel's experience not only because this experience is based considerably on the manipulation of the visible and the invisible, but also because the General controls power and the image he projects by manipulating what is visible. Thus, there is a correlation between characterization and character and also between them and technique. When the General actually sees his own death (that of his double) in the first chapter, the experience changes him profoundly. This anecdote is described by means of a repetition of the verb "to see." The intensity of this experience is based on the fact that he *sees* death. Just as death becomes a reality for the General after he sees it, he confides only in reality as he can observe it, and becomes a victim of the circumstances he has created through his power. When he falls in love with Manuela Sánchez, he attempts to attract her with the visible manifestation of his power. Logically, the maximum gift for his maximum love, then, is the most impressive visual spectacle possible. Thus, his gift for Manuela Sánchez is a comet.

Maintenance of power is determined by the General's ability to manipulate the visible and the invisible. After a potential assassin fails to kill him, the General not only orders the man put to death, but more significantly in the context of his own understanding of the importance of the visible, he orders that the different parts of the assassin's body be exhibited throughout the country, thus providing a visible manifestation of the consequences of questioning the General's power. When he feels the necessity for exerting maximum control of his power, he visibly observes its functioning. This also explains the General's bizarre insistence in observing the milking of the cows each morning. On the other hand, when his power is threatened by the church (it denies sainthood to his mother), the General takes direct control of the situation, declares "civil sainthood" for his mother, and, given the seriousness of the situation, visibly oversees the fulfillment of his orders. In one description the General is portrayed as most content when he has a complete view of his country through his window. Similarly, he considers himself less responsible for that which he does not see. He feels no compunction about ordering the massacre of two thousand children, because he does not observe the actual killing, and the brutal maneuvers of Sáenz de la Barra are of little consequence to him because they are covert. Being aware of this importance of the visible, one of the General's officials suggests that Sáenz might be eliminated from the government if there were some way the General could *see* the atrocities taking place.

The question of the visible and the invisible and its relation to the novel's main theme, power, is also elaborated through the presence of the sea ("mar") in the novel. As the superb visible object in the General's daily life, the "mar" is his most treasured possession. The "mar" is first mentioned in the first chapter when, after a reiteration of the verb "to see," the narrator-discoverer ends a sentence on the third page of the novel as follows: "vimos los cráteres muertos de ásperas cenizas de luna de llanura sin término donde había estado el mar" (7) ("we saw the dead craters of harsh moon ash on the endless plain where the sea had been," 9). Early in the novel such a reference to the "mar" seems inexplicable. In the context of the novel and the General's concept of power, it is understood that, since the General conceives of his "mar" as lost, it is naturally perceived as such by the citizenry, which is totally indoctrinated by him. In the first chapter the "mar" also becomes closely associated with his window, and from this point his window and his "mar" are inseparable in the novel. Technically, this association is established through the use of the preposition "de" ("of"): "oyó por la ventana abierta del mar los tambores lejanos las taitas tristes . . ." (25) ("through the open windows facing the sea he could hear the distant drums . . . ," 25–26). When the General condemns some political prisoners to death, international pressure is placed upon him to annul the order. In such moments of crisis, he contemplates from his window. As he gradually loses control of his power, he turns to his window more often. At the end of the fifth chapter, decrepit and in his hundredth year of power, he goes to his window and watches the sea, seemingly observing his very loss of power: "iba viendo pasar el mismo mar por las ventanas . . ." (216) ("he went along seeing as he passed the same sea through the windows. . . ," 201).

His window, his "mar," and his power become so intimately associated that the General insists upon maintaining possession of his window and "mar" as persistently as he does with reference to maintaining his power. When he is in the process of losing his power, he is adament about not losing his "mar." In one of his extensive dialogues with an ambassador, he defends his position concerning the sea:

trying to explain to him that he could take anything he wanted except the sea of my windows, just imagine, what would I do all alone in this big building if I couldn't look out now as always at this time at what looks like a marsh in flames, what would I do without the December winds that sneak in barking through the broken windowpanes, how could I live without the green flashes of the lighthouse, I who abandoned my misty barrens and enlisted to the agony of fever in the tumult of the federalist war, and don't you think that I did it out of patriotism as the dictionary says, or from the spirit of adventure, or least of all because I gave a shit about federal principles which God keep in his holy kingdom, no my dear Wilson, I did it all so I could get to know the sea. . . . (187–88)

He has a similar response later for Ambassador Stevenson. When yet another ambassador attempts to make a deal, the General once more refuses. The sign that the General has lost his power is the selling of his sea at the end of the novel: "I granted them the right to make use of our territorial waters in the way they considered best for the interests of humanity and peace among peoples, with the understanding that said cession not only included the physical waters visible from the window of his bedroom to the horizon but everything that is understood by sea in the broadest sense, or, the flora and fauna belonging to said waters . . ." (230–31). The General has lost his maximum view and all that was significant for him:

"they carried off everything that had been the reasons for my wars and the motive of his power . . ." (231).

The four levels of the novel's structure as described above are functional in the elaboration of the novel's themes. The opening of the original situation into the General's story provides a complete characterization of the General not limited by traditional subordination of the narration to the requirements of space and time. The latter are subordinate, in *The Autumn of the Patriarch,* to the act of narrating itself. The opening of the sentence supports this first opening technically, and is a specific device that provides for a progressively more elaborate textual presentation of the story. The opening of the narrative focus provides for a multiplicity of views of the General, and this is significant not only in the complexity and completeness of the characterization of him, but also in establishing the novel's tone—the humor that is fundamental to the experience of the novel. On the final level, the opening of a seen reality into a confluence of the visible and the invisible, the experience of the novel becomes similar to the principle theme it develops: the illusion of reality and power. To a considerable extent, the universalization of this theme through specific techniques creates the reader's experience. Although the cycle of novels focused on Macondo is finished, the universal experience created in *The Autumn of the Patriarch* is a continuation of the transcendent regionalism so evident in García Márquez's previous work, especially *One Hundred Years of Solitude.*

Chapter Seven
Chronicle of a Death Foretold (1981) and Journalism

The Writer as Journalist

Journalism has been a constant presence in García Márquez's literary and personal biography. It was journalism, in the early years in Cartagena and Barranquilla, that provided him with the opportunity to earn a living with the pen. As has been suggested in the discussion of "A Tale of a Castaway," journalism was essential to the development of García Márquez's fiction (see chapter 2). García Márquez has stated that "journalism helped maintain contact with reality, which is essential to literature."[1]

García Márquez the novelist has gained far more from journalism than just "contact with reality." There were crucial initial lessons in writing for the general public—and the related fictionalization of a reader. Certain techniques considered basic to journalism have become constant in García Márquez's fiction: the creation of a high level of interest from the very first lines of a text; the use of journalistic details.

García Márquez also maintains that he became a good journalist by reading literature.[2] The broad range of fictional styles and techniques with which he became acquainted during the early years on the coast undoubtedly afforded new possibilities for his journalism. A reading of his journalistic writings during this period, in fact, shows a writer experimenting with a variety of styles, techniques, and genres. Both the enormous volume of García Márquez's journalism and its intimate relationship to his fiction make his journalistic writings essential to a complete study of his work.

The publication of *Chronicle of a Death Foretold* showcased García Márquez the journalist. The journalist-fiction writer penned a story of love and revenge, based on events that had happened to some of

García Márquez's best friends of thirty years before. Consequently, journalists poured into Sucre, the coastal town where all this took place, in order to interview the surviving characters. The perennially vague line distinguishing fact and fiction, the journalist and the novelist, had been made even more nebulous.

Chronicle of a Death Foretold

The novel's first line, like that of most of García Márquez's novels and most good journalism, is arresting: "On the day they were going to kill him, Santiago Nasar got up at five-thirty in the morning to wait for the boat the bishop was coming on."[3] The author has been interested in detective novels since his youth; announcing the death in the first line makes this a kind of mystery novel in reverse. The reader knows the outcome from the first line and continues reading—with interests very similar to those aroused in the detective novel—to see the death consummated, which it will be, and, more importantly, to see *how* it will happen. The circumstances surrounding Santiago Nasar's death become increasingly more incredible: everyone in the town knew he was going to die except Santiago himself. Yet no one says anything.

Perhaps even more incredible then García Márquez's fiction, however, are the facts. The magazine *Al Día* reported the following story:

In the municipality of Sucre (of the department of the same name), the elders still remember with horror the rainy morning of January 22, 1951, in which a young man from Sucre, Cayetano Gentile Chimento, twenty-two years old, medical student at the Javeriana University of Bogotá and heir of the town's largest fortune, fell butchered by machete, innocent victim of a confused duel of honor, and without knowing for sure why he was dying. Cayetano was killed by Víctor and Joaquín Chica Salas, whose sister Margarita, married the previous day with Miguel Reyes Palencia and returned to her family by her husband the same night of the marriage, accused Cayetano of being the author of the disgrace that had prevented her being a virgin at her marriage.[4]

These grisly events form the anecdotal base for García Márquez's fiction. The novel consists of five chapters which are not exactly a "chronicle" if one holds to the dictionary definition of this genre—a chronological record of historical events. The first chapter recounts

the morning of the assassination by the two brothers, who are called
Pedro and Pablo Vicario in the novel. The second relates the background of the relationship between future husband and wife, Bayardo
San Román and Angela Vicario. This chapter carries the pair's story
forward to the evening of the wedding. The third chapter deals with
the evening of the wedding, the night before Santiago Nasar's death.
There is a temporal move forward in the fourth chapter, which tells
of the events subsequent to the tragedy, such as the autopsy for
Santiago Nasar and Angela Vicario's life during the years after the
failed marriage. The last chapter returns to the chronology of events
surrounding the actual assassination, culminating in a detailed and
graphic description of the death.

Several elements woven into the novel's texture modify objective
reality, despite the inclusion of much objective detail.[5] These include
dreams and premonitions which are incorrectly interpreted, the ambiguous and flexible distance between the occurrence of events and
their reconstruction, and events that seem to carry a symbolic meaning, such as the rains, the insomnia, the dreams, and the odors that
are called moral indicators.

There would seem to be an underlying system here that provides
a profound and coherent understanding of things, but there is not.
Rather, as in all of García Márquez's work, life is determined by
inexplicable forces and irrational acts. The narrator explains that
attempts at rational explanation fall short, although the judge who
was assigned to Nasar's case approached it with the intention of
finding a rational interpretation: "Nadie podía entender tantas coin-
cidencias funestas. El juez instructor que vino de Riohacha debió
sentirlas sin atreverse a admitirlas, pues su interés de darles una
explicación racional era evidente en el sumario" (20) ("No one could
understand such fatal coincidences. The investigating judge who
came from Riohacha must have sensed them without daring to admit
it, for his impulse to give a rational explanation was obvious in his
report," 12). The narrator, nevertheless, does not demonstrate an
interest in rational explanation, or in offering speculation as to how
things happened as they did.

One of García Márquez's basic techniques for the creation of
ambiguity is the use of detailed particularity concerning irrevelant
matters on the one hand, and vagueness about points of real importance. The basic procedure is like that journalism which abounds
in detailed facts, but fails to provide the broad picture of the events

at hand. One result is a series of questions which cannot be answered: who really violated Angela?; did Victoria Guzmán (the cook) and her daughter know of the assassination plan or not?; did the narrator's sister, Margot, know of the plot?; what was the weather really like the day of Santiago Nasar's demise? Several other questions without a solution arise.

The narrative situation is also a source of considerable ambiguity. A first-person narrator-investigator tells the story. He returns to the town after the story's central event to tell it in retrospection. His lack of omniscience, of course, makes the matter of interpretation problematical from the beginning. Since he did not witness the events, his project is to accumulate, organize, and relate the anecdotes. The book is a process of investigation in which the reader is informed by the narrator of his own procedures at the same time that he supposedly reveals the key facts. The problem, however, is that the procedure—the accumulation of facts—overshadows the important revelations, which never come forth.

The text consists of individual versions of what happened, which, in their entirety, result in the "dizque" ("it is said") of popular knowledge. Reviewing these individuals cited directly by the narrator, one can note a total of thirty-seven characters who contribute to this "chronicle" of the narrator-investigator. The characters who are most quoted as sources of information are, in descending order, the following: Angela Vicario (directly quoted twelve times), Cristo Bedoya (nine times), Pablo Vicario (seven times), and Margot (seven times). The narrator-investigator's total "record" for his chronicle consists of nine citations from the written record and a total of 102 quotations from the thirty-seven characters.

Contrary to what has been announced in the title, this novel is not a chronicle: the narrative situation in effect subverts any historical pretension underlying the literariness of this verbal construction. Technically speaking, the most authoritative voice in the novel is that of Angela Vicario, whom the narrator quotes twelve times. The narrator thus gives precedence, ironically, to the version of the story given by precisely the person investigated. In the end, there is neither a historian nor an authoritative voice in the text: the concept of authority itself becomes enigmatic.

In addition to the questioning of authority, *Chronicle of a Death Foretold* permits the observation of other ideologemes—narrative unities of a socially symbolic type.[6] The novel turns upon itself without going beyond its own fixed ideological limits, that is, the limits of the town's mentality. The language and boundaries of this ideology are a fundamentally medieval tradition—a matter of honor. The bride is rejected, the murder is conceived, and then allowed to be executed—despite the full knowledge of everyone in this town—because of the entire town's tacit acceptance of a medieval conception of human relationships. The novel's structure (the development of the predetermined action) as well as the process in the town (the events that the town's citizenry witness) correspond to a world in which the development of things is determined by a hierarchical and static vision of reality.

Class differences play an important role in the development of events.[7] The Nasars represent an upper class that distinguishes them from the rest of the town's citizenry by origins and by money. For both reasons they are hated in the town. They have become affluent in the town while everyone else has languished in poverty. On the one hand, there is potential jealousy on the part of the townspeople because of Santiago Nasar's superior class status. On the other hand, he is such a handsome and financially comfortable candidate for any woman, it is logical that he is the cause of jealousy and envy among the other young men in the town. His fiancée is Flora Miguel, from one of the town's other affluent families. The narrator's sister thinks about Flora Miguel's good fortune in having Santiago as a future husband, and she provides the reader with one woman's estimation of him: "I suddenly realized that there couldn't have been a better catch than him. Just imagine: handsome, a man of his word, and with a fortune of his own at the age of twenty-one" (18). The confluence of economic, personal, and possibly even political interests makes the true dynamics underlying Santiago Nasar's death ambiguous and, in the end, an unresolvable matter.

William Gass has suggested that *Chronicle of a Death Foretold* is not told, but literally pieced together.[8] The novel is not about Santiago's death, which is already established in the first sentence. Rather, its real focus is the process of the story's coming into being, the author's placing the numerous pieces together. As in *The Autumn of the Patriarch,* the act of writing dominates over the anecdotal content. The anticipated period at the end of the sentence in the dictator novel has as its equivalent the final period anticipated and foretold in this novel, the actual death which takes place in the last chapter.

This novel shares other characteristics with the previous fiction. In addition to the fact that the opening line is effective in eliciting the reader's attention and immediately involving him in the book, as in the other novels, the beginning reflects other of García Márquez's interests. One of the constants is the overwhelming presence of death, a presence also manifested from the beginning. "I've seen a corpse for the first time," the boy states in the opening line of the first monologue of *Leafstorm*. The initial lines of *One Hundred Years of Solitude* evoke the image of Colonel Aureliano Buendía dying before the firing squad. *The Autumn of the Patriarch* opens with a description of a rotting palace containing a corpse. Several of the short stories begin similarly.[9] *Chronicle of a Death Foretold* is a book which creates an apocalypse predetermined from the beginning, like *One Hundred Years of Solitude* and *The Autumn of the Patriarch*.

With this novel García Márquez attains the perfect symbiosis of the writer-as-novelist and the writer-as-journalist.[10] One level of this synthesis is attained by the use of journalistic technique, using the chronicle as an ostensible model. Another level is the use of a real-life drama, presented by the narrator-investigator. The confluence of reality and fiction reaches an acute point of ambiguity when the narrator inserts García Márquez by mentioning the author's wife, Mercedes Barcha:

In the course of the investigations for this chronicle I recovered numerous marginal experiences, among them the free recollections of Bayardo San Roman's sisters, whose velvet dresses with great butterfly wings. . . . Many knew that in the confusion of the bash I had proposed marriage to Mercedes Barcha as soon as she finished primary school. . . . (43)

In much fiction the use of the author's name functions as a reminder of the work's fictionality; in this novel the mention of Mercedes and her marriage to García Márquez contributes to the effect of all the characters and actions being a part of the real world, the writing of journalism. As when reading the newspaper, the reader of this novel must carefully select among the numerous details, many of which are unimportant. In fact, much of the most detailed information to which the reader has access is irrelevant. The process of selection of this text's creator has been done by the hand of a journalist, not a novelist.

Chronicle of a Death Foretold is the product of a writer with the ability to successfully manipulate several genres: the novel, journalism, and detective fiction. García Márquez uses some of the conventions of each to author a work which, like *The Incredible and Sad Tale of Innocent Eréndira and Her Heartless Grandmother,* is not a book of profound resonance, but a superb entertainment.

Journalism

García Márquez's career in journalism stretches from the late 1940s to the present, although there have been unproductive periods, usually when he has been preoccupied exclusively with writing fiction. In the context of this total career as a novelist, the most interesting period of journalism was his preprofessional days as a novelist, from the late 1940s to the mid-1950s. The journalism of these years, compiled in a volume entitled *Textos costeños,* will be the central focus of the remainder of this chapter.

The journalistic pieces which García Márquez published from 1948 to 1952 would be of interest even if they did not happen to become the first writings of a Nobel Prize winning author. They are a fascinating review of the period, including regular commentary on such persons as President Truman, the films of the times, and the advent of the hydrogen bomb. They provide a sense of daily life in Colombia—many cultural and political events of no lasting value—and a sense of the times as seen from Colombia. They often carry the fresh stamp of innocence, the mark of a twenty-year-old writer who is writing before public postures or pretense became important.

During this period he published over four hundred short pieces, on a wide variety of topics and in several genres. Exact classification of all this writing in traditional genre definitions would be extremely difficult and probably pointless, but the articles range from political commentary to fiction. They include notes that might be called "social commentary"—not necessarily social criticism, but observations concerning local, national, and world events. This social commentary is the most common content of Grácia Márquez's column. Some of the journalism is cultural or literary commentary. Again, "commentary" is more appropriate than a term such as "literary criticism"; the publication of a new book more often elicited praise of the author and affirmation of friendship with this fine person than an attempt at objective review of the book. A considerable portion of García Márquez's total journalistic production is fiction. This writing includes short stories, short fictional anecdotes, and even short sections of fiction intended to become a novel. This type of writing sometimes eludes categorization: a news item which the journalist received over the teletype could be converted into an anecdote with a substantial portion of fiction and artistic transformation.

Affinities to the later fiction and direct origins of it are present in this journalism. In some pieces the similarities are reflected in a distantly comparable idea or vaguely reminiscent tone. Some themes are the direct origins of García Márquez's central preoccupations in his later novelistic career. The investigative scholar of García Márquez will find these writings rich material: such pieces as an overt attempt at imitating Kafka, his praise of Faulkner, and short "Notes for a Novel" (with characters from the later Macondo) are definitive proof of much of what has been speculated on the basis of interviews and analysis of García Márquez's later fiction.

These articles demonstrate that his interest in detective novels far predates the publication of *Chronicle of a Death Foretold*. The novel showed an awareness of the genre; the early journalism indicates that García Márquez was fascinated with detective novels from a very early age. In June 1950, García Márquez published in his regular column a "Cuentecillo policiaco" (A little police story), an imitation of detective fiction. A woman, identified as "Señora A," is surprised with the discovery of the corpse of "Señor B" at her door. A mystery arises: "Señora A" had spoken with "Señor B" at five in the afternoon, but the doctor is absolutely positive that the man has been dead for eight hours, that is, since ten in the morning. The police investigator, confronted with these grossly contradictory facts, smokes three entire packages of cigarettes and drinks sixteen cups of black coffee. He goes to bed thinking: "This cannot be. This only happens in detective stories."

García Márquez's first written acknowledgment of this genre, like the novel he would publish thirty-one years later, approaches detective fiction with some distance and playfulness. The insistence on revealing precise times for every action from the story's second line is the most obvious exaggeration of the presence of the singularly important facts of the detective story. The caricature of the detective at the end of the story makes it an obvious parody. Successful parody requires a sound knowledge of the genre; García Márquez also demonstrates an acquaintance with such stories in an article published in July 1951, entitled: "Un cadáver en el ropero" (A Cadaver in

the Closet). He discusses his assertion that the most common occurrence in these novels is for a cadaver to be discovered in a closet
the evening of 31 December. He points out, ironically, how on no
other day of the year do so many people die in closets. The remainder
of the short article deals with the rarity of the fulfilling of this
fictional convention in real life.

García Márquez's most serious exposition on detective fiction,
published in October 1952, deals with the enigmas of this genre.
These novels, according to García Márquez, are better studied by
"literary detectives" than by "literary critics" because they have an
attraction which no academic can explain. These novels are a habitual
vice like smoking or betting, but a bad habit which the author
defends. He points out that even President Franklin D. Roosevelt
practiced this vice, because he read several police novels during the
Yalta Conference. García Márquez's fascination with logic and rational processes is expressed in his observation that in these novels
the enigma always destroys itself, and it does so with something as
simple and foolish as logic. He suggests two exceptions to this rule:
Dickens's *The Mystery of Edwin Drood* and Sophocles' *Oedipus Rex*.
The Dickens novel is an exception because the author died before
he could finish the novel—or solve the enigma. The case of Oedipus
Rex is more difficult to explain: it is the only example in detective
literature in which the detective, after the complete investigation,
discovers that he himself is the assassin of his father.

Even though his major fiction shows little traces of this genre,
the interest in this type of fiction spans some thirty years, from
these virtually unknown journalistic pieces to the publication of
Chronicle of a Death Foretold. A review of the early journalism reveals
several other links between this period and the later fiction. Some
of these connections are direct: a statement or reference from the
journalism will appear later in the fiction. Other links are more
indirect, such as an idea, theme, or technique which will appear in
a story or novel.

The direct references relate to such items as José Arcadio Buendía's
humorous pronouncement in the first chapter of *One Hundred Years
of Solitude* that the earth is "round, like an orange." In an article
published in October 1950, García Márquez laments the progressively scientific view of the world, and proposes that the world was
conceived in a more poetic fashion until someone declared "The
world is round!" This is an example of how an idea he originally

used in his journalism appears directly later. The origin of the manuscript in *One Hundred Years of Solitude* is one of the novel's most memorable surprises. There are at least two references to ancient manuscripts in this writing. The same word used in Spanish for the original manuscript in *One Hundred Years of Solitude—pergamino—* is the subject of one of García Márquez's articles written in June 1948. He comments on the exhibition of a curious *pergamino* in a museum in New York. An article about another manuscript published later (June 1950) has several resonances of *One Hundred Years of Solitude:* "The cable dated from New York says that Dr. Guido Kirch has discovered, after ten years of study of an ancient manuscript nine-hundred years old, that Adam and Eve had a daughter named Naoba."[11] The importance of both the manuscript and the Bible becomes apparent in the later novel.

Some of the articles relate directly to the short stories published later. An incident mentioned with reference to the Mississippi River relates so directly to the story "The Last Voyage of the Ghost Ship" that this article could well be the initial catalyst for the later creation of the story. In this article, published in April 1951, García Márquez mentions having heard the story of a "ghost ship" ("barco fantasma") on the Mississippi. This empty ship floated along the Mississippi with its lights out. Like the ghost ship in "The Last Voyage of the Ghost Ship," this ship seems to have supernatural powers: "con la rueda lateral girando en virtud de una fuerza sobrenatural" (638).

One humorous incident in "The Handsomest Drowned Man in the World" is the naming of the drowned man. He is named when one of the inhabitants suddenly declares: "He has the face of someone named Esteban." García Márquez wrote an article in February 1952 dealing with naming. This piece, entitled "Hay que parecerse al nombre" ("One Must Be Like the Name"), is devoted to the matter of the relationship between a person's name and this person's physical traits. The article begins with the author recalling having heard a remark quite similar to the naming of Esteban in "The Handsomest Drowned Man in the World": "Tenía cara de llamarse Roberto, pero se llamaba José" ("He had the face of someone named Roberto, but his name was José," 716).

The link between Kafka and García Márquez's early fiction can be made direct with a reading of these articles. The most interesting piece of writing in this context is a "Caricature of Kafka," a brief parody of Kafka's writing, published in August 1950. This piece contains several elements easily recognizable by the reader of Kafka: the characters are identified by letters rather than names; the protagonist has just completed a trip throughout the night; the environs are of cold steel and ugly modernity; the protagonist's effort in crossing a bridge is thwarted by an official who is a part of a vast hierarchy; the protagonist suffers from an initial indecision and ultimate failure.

Nightmares which relate directly to both García Márquez's initial stories and Kafka appear with some regularity in the early journalism. It is obvious that during this period García Márquez was fascinated with the subject of nightmares. One of his articles published in June 1950, entitled "Una parrafada" (A paragraph), refers to "pesadillas kafkianas" ("Kafkaesque nightmares"). It is only a passing remark in the context of an article which communicates one of his rare moments of boredom with everyday life and writing and perhaps even a little frustration with the routines. The following month, July 1950, he published a brief fictional anecdote titled "Pesadillas" (Nightmares) whose central focus is nightmares. In this story a man enters a newspaper office and offers his nightmares to the director. The entire story is the dialogue between the two men, with the visitor attempting to convince the director of the value of publishing his dreams in the newspaper. It is a particularly notable story when one takes into account García Márquez's attempts at creating an "other reality" in his short stories published during the 1948–52 period (see chapter 2). Another fictional anecdote published later the same year (October 1950), entitled "Un profesional de la pesadilla" (A Nightmare Professional), deals with a character who is a nightmare specialist. This man, Nathaniel, spends twenty years concentrating on having the best nightmares possible. He purposely induces indigestion and nervousness in order to produce the strangest and most "difficult" nightmares. The story describes his numerous techniques and the exotic nightmares they produce.

Much of the journalism published during this period does not necessarily relate to the later fiction in such a direct fashion as the type of articles cited above. Rather, this journalism shares themes that have a regular presence in his fiction. A reading of the journalism confirms that García Márquez has been constantly preoccupied with such themes as death, the rational and the nonrational, the effects of modern science and technology, the common man, and insanity.

As has been pointed out in the discussion of García Márquez's fiction in the previous chapters, there are humanistic and antiscience underpinnings to many of these stories. Skeptical and critical of the human consequences of modern science and technology, and the concurrent "progress" which these advances promise, García Márquez has been a defender of profoundly human values. He portrays the common man and his struggle to maintain dignity, for example, in several of the stories in *Big Mama's Funeral* (see chapter 3). These deeply humanistic aspects of García Márquez's writing are consistently present in the early journalism. Several of his articles, dealing with a variety of topics, include comments which reveal his skepticism of modern sicence. An article entitled "Sobre el fin del mundo" (On the end of the world) published in February 1950, is a criticism of one of science's most destructive inventions ever, the hydrogen bomb. In a much lighter note published in February 1952, he defends traditional human relationships as opposed to changes brought about by technology. This piece, titled "El amor por teléfono" (Love by telephone), deals with all the romanticism lost between lovers who converse by telephone instead of observing the Latin-American tradition of exchanging intimate words through the beloved's open window. García Márquez laments the loss of this more human and personal mode of communication. A similar line of thought appears in an article "Se acabaron los barberos" (No more barbers), in which García Márquez expresses his regret over the disappearance of the traditional small-town barber. Modern barbers of the city, according to García Márquez, are far too antiseptic and scientific.

Concurrent with the attack on the dehumanizing aspects of science and technology is the author's interest in the common man. He celebrates the value of the man on the street or other socially undistinguished persons with whom García Márquez had daily contact. Many of the persons who were exalted in García Márquez's newspaper column were not the typical material for such commentary: the black woman, the Indian, the little boy who was always around the newspaper office. In an article titled "El hombre de la calle" (The man in the street), published in May 1950, García Márquez claims that the "man in the street" is his central concern as a journalist. This statement is justified by articles such as the one titled "el hombre que no ríe" (The man who doesn't laugh), published in May 1950: García Márquez describes a peasant he had just met. In "La horma de sus zapatos" (The shoe's last, September 1950), García

Márquez exalts shoe repairmen, maintaining that all of them have a little of the philosopher. A light note published in October of the same year, "¿Dónde están los borrachos?" (Where are the drunks?), describes the entertaining and harmless town drunk, another of the picturesque characters that García Márquez regrets to observe disappearing from small towns. Journalists in Colombia with regular columns such as that of García Márquez frequently devote their space to praising (or criticizing) politicians or the government projects which the politicians support. García Márquez, in contrast, rarely even mentions politicians by name. Rather, he writes an article about a little boy, Bartolo, whom everyone at the newspaper office had seen regularly on a nearby street. García Márquez writes of the special experience Bartolo will have flying the kite for which all the employees in the office contributed money.

One of the most consistent themes in García Márquez's fiction is death. As has been pointed out in the discussion of *Chronicle of a Death Foretold,* much of his fiction is structured around a death. Death also has a constant presence in the early journalism. One of the most revealing processes concerning his attitude about death is an article written upon the death of George Bernard Shaw. The first sentence of the article reads as follows: "Mr. George Bernard Shaw—¡siempre tan oportuno!—escogió para morirse el dos de noviembre que es, sin duda, el día más apropiado para hacer esa incómoda diligencia" (488) ("Mr. George Bernard Shaw—always so timely—chose the second of November to die, which is undoubtedly the most appropriate day to take care of this uncomfortable duty"). November 2, of course, is All Soul's Day. By using the phrase "incómoda diligencia" ("uncomfortable duty") to describe Shaw's death, García Márquez underplays the importance of this act, in an even lightly humorous tone. After praising the Irish writer, García Márquez states that Shaw's death is something "too serious to be taken literally." This is an attitude which pervades García Márquez's writing: death never seems to signify the literal end of life. Thus, characters such as Melquíades in *One Hundred Years of Solitude* can "return" from death to participate in life with those still alive.

The phenomenon of "muertos vivos"—"dead-alive persons"—which appears in the first stories, is also developed in this journalism. An article titled "Los funerales de Jim Gersnhart" (Jim Gersnhart's funeral), published in June 1951, deals with an American who organized his own funeral procession before his death. It is a story which García Márquez apparently received from the wire service at the newspaper. The American, Jim Gersnhart, attended an elaborate funeral service for himself. Afterward, he stored his coffin in the basement, ready for his real death. García Márquez re-creates this admittedly bizarre anecdote and concludes that Mr. Gersnhart was "scientifically alive and technically dead." This is precisely the "dead-alive" type of oxymoron which García Márquez employs in his stories. He draws a careful comparison of the actions of live persons and dead persons in "Más nos valiera estar muertos" (We would be better off dead, April 1952). This somewhat light article concludes that the dead understand what those alive are doing, but not vice versa. Consequently, one is more privileged dead than alive.

Events and situations in García Márquez's fiction sometimes defy rational explanation. They question the usefulness of man's rational capabilities or, similarly, seem to view insanity with a certain sympathy. Some of the journalism is an actual defense of insanity. Again, the "defense" is set forth in a light tone. García Márquez writes about "El derecho de volverse loco" (The right to go crazy) in an article published immediately before the carnival season in January 1950. After a full year of the "fastidious" necessity of sanity, according to the author, everyone is well deserving of the right to go crazy. García Márquez writes with considerable discomfort of the news that in the United States a drug against insanity has been invented (May 1950). He proposes that his drug, if successful, will be detrimental: the George Bernard Shaws, the Aldous Huxleys, and the William Faulkners of the world will cease to exist in this new world of absolute sanity.

A considerable portion of the journalism which García Márquez published during this 1948–52 period was fiction. The space which he had at his disposition in a column, of course, was much more limited than that traditionally accorded to the short story. Some of the pieces are very brief short stories; others could be more adequately described as "fictional anecdotes." These anecdotes tell a story, but without the structure and development of the traditional short story. The pieces that are actual short stories, logically enough, are often quite similar to the fiction of that period which is usually considered his first stories (see chapter 2). "El bebedor de Coca-Cola," (Coca-Cola drinkers), for example, which he published in May 1952, is a first-person narration which characterizes one man. The description seems to be a futile attempt at creating an extraordinary man. The protagonist's most outstanding characteristic is that he is an obsessive drinker of Coca-Cola. Rather than creating a truly memorable soft-drink addict, the young García Márquez explains directly: "Resultaba muy fácil darse cuenta de que era un hombre extraordinario" (755) ("It was very easy to realize that he was an extraordinary man").

"Elegía" (Elegy, September 1952) is a much better written story; it could well have been included in anthologies and volumes of García Márquez's first stories. In addition to its quality, it would fit in such a book because of the situation it presents: a man who dies in strange circumstances. The protagonist dies suddenly from having eaten a plate of clams. In typical García Márquez fashion of dealing with death, the dying is described in a peculiar way: "Aquello era tan inusitado y repentino, que Oliverio no había acabado de darse cuenta de lo que le había ocurrido, cuando lo metieron en el ataúd, tres o cuatro horas después" (817) ("It was so unexpected and sudden, that Oliverio didn't realize what had happened when they put him in the coffin, three or four hours later"). "Elegía" develops the story of its protagonist, albeit in only two pages. Much of the fiction published between 1948 and 1952, unlike this story, does not develop a clear story line or a well defined character.

A considerable portion of what could be identified as fiction published in newspapers does not aspire to be a traditional short story. Rather, it is a highly fictionalized elaboration of a newspaper story. These newspaper stories originated from the international wire service to which García Márquez had access as an employee of the newspaper. The typical piece of this sort begins with a reference to some story that was received over the wire service (the "cable" in Spanish). An initial reading of a few of these anecdotes from the wire service might lead a reader to conclude that García Márquez is relaying or retelling human-interest-type stories as received from abroad. A more careful review of the complete set of some two dozen articles, however, reveals a transformation of the basic anecdotal material in a way that reflects, above all, the pen of a young Gabriel García Márquez. A first step in the process of creating fiction—selection—is, of course, controlled entirely by García Márquez: of the hundreds of wire-service stories received during these years, García Márquez selected both the stories he would retell and which details of these stories he would emphasize. The author's choice of material naturally reflects those themes and aspects of his writing already discussed in the context of his fiction: the incredible or fantastic event, the decadence of the modern world, those special attitudes about death, a skepticism about purely rational methods of interpreting phenomena, and others. Beyond these matters of selection are those concerning how the story is transformed from its original wire service version into a fictional one. The account which García Márquez published does contain a base in fact, but the elaboration of the story makes it fiction. Any reader can conclude that these stories are indeed fictional accounts because of the fact that they contain numerous details and comments that no wire service would carry.

The difference between a brief wire service story and the inventive fiction of García Márquez is particularly ostentatious in some of the stories. In "Fricciones a la Bella Durmiente" (Rubbing medications for Sleeping Beauty, March 1950), the basic anecdotal material received through the wire service is as follows: an adolescent Italian by the name of Mirella Petrini has been asleep for over two hundred hours and, consequently, doctors are experimenting with various rubbing medications and injections to awaken her. García Márquez's story is considerably more imaginative: the young girl has "extraordinary" beauty; the author admits that the wire service said nothing of her home, but then explains how it is possible to imagine its "ample terrace" and other features; he goes on to speculate about the young girl's impoverished childhood. All this speculation and imagination lead to García Márquez's transformation of a medical curiosity into a tale of romance: Mirella becomes a modern version of Sleeping Beauty. The doctors attempting to resuscitate Mirella— probably heroes in the international press releases—become the villains in García Márquez's version of the story. Their ointments and injections represent the destruction of a myth.

The anecdotal material in "Los ayunos del padre Walterson" (Father Walterson's fast) is the fast of a British vicar, who proclaims that he will not eat until the formation of a national committee to facilitate a rapprochement between the United States and the Soviet Union. After García Márquez explains this situation, he uses the remaining two pages to speculate in an entirely fictional manner about the Reverend Mr. Walterson and the world scenario. In many of these pieces the exact location of the line that divides the daily international news from García Márquez's invention is impossible to fix. Both the real event and invention are elements of these pieces.

Certain pieces of fiction from this 1948–52 period can be classified into specific coherent groupings that provide valuable insights into the formative steps of the later fiction. A set of ten short fictional pieces which could be identified as the "Marquesa" fiction was an early exercise in wild invention. These pieces were published at intervals between April and June of 1950. The story, which has little development of plot and action, deals with a Marquesa and her husband Boris, who seems to be in India. In reality, only the first two pieces deal specifically with the story of this aristocratic pair. The first tells of the gift elephant which Boris sends from India to his Marquesa in Germany. The animal speaks German upon arrival. In the second story it is revealed that Boris, in fact, sends the Marquesa an exotic gift each week. This particular week she receives an ancient chair from him. Once this basic situation is established, this "Marquesa" series becomes even more inventive, as the author plays with his characters. In one piece, for example, García Márquez tells of a visit to his office by a woman who claims to be the Marquesa. He maintains in a published letter to the Marquesa that he needs to put an end to her existence, but cannot make himself do so. The tongue-in-cheek saga continues with letters and adventures from a variety of sources.

The concluding piece of this "Marquesa" set of fictions contains valuable statements about García Márquez, the novice fiction writer of 1950. Titled "El final necesario" (The Necessary End), this article is the author's reflections on the total experience of the "Marquesa" series. The article represents a serious affirmation of the right of invention. The author says of the Marquesa, for example, "creo en ella" ("I believe in her"). He explains that this invention had served a vital function in his journalistic writing: it was, in his own words, an "escape valve" for his literary interests. This experience also contributed to García Márquez's awareness of the all-important matter of fictionalizing a reader. The publication of this series of fictions provoked a surprising response from the reading public. García Márquez received letters from numerous persons, communications ranging from suggested directions of his story to criticisms of the whole idea. One irate reader complained, according to García Márquez, that the entire set of articles had become "disorderly." All of this response was a most practical lesson in developing an awareness of the reader and the ability to manipulate this fictionalized entity.

Another valuable set of writings are those that could be called the "La Sierpe" series. They were published in December 1952, when García Márquez's career as a writer of fiction was in a relatively advanced stage. They are seven short—less than a page—vignettes about a region in the Caribbean coastal region called La Sierpe. They are like the physical setting and other background for a novel to be developed. The author introduces La Sierpe as a land of enchantment and witchcraft, abounding in legends about the past and the fantastic in the present. There are still rumors about a kind old Spanish lady who inhabited La Sierpe, a "gran mamá" who recalls the short story published a decade later with the same title. It is not difficult to relate La Sierpe to the Macondo that will be created soon after the publication of La Sierpe, and which was written more or less concurrently with it. The location and legendary overtones are typical of the later literature of Macondo.

There is also a set of fictional pieces of this period which not only relate to Macondo, but which appear to be a portion of the first drafts of the Macondo fiction. This writing, which will be identified here as the "Pre-Macondo fiction" for the sake of convenience, has the greatest potential for careful study by the scholar of all that was written during the 1948–52 period. This Pre-Macondo fiction is identified as "Apuntes para una novela" (Notes for a novel) by the author. The first of these "notes" was published in June 1950, and could almost be a few paragraphs from a poorly edited version of *One Hundred Years of Solitude*. Titled "La Hija del Coronel" (The Colonel's Daughter), it features such characters as Colonel Aureliano Buendía and Remedios. It is basically a brief passage about knowledge, getting to know the world, like the first chapter of *One Hundred Years of Solitude*. Rebecca is the character who gains understanding in this case. Locations of utmost importance in *One Hundred Years of Solitude,* the town and the home, are also very significant for Rebecca here. "El Hijo del Coronel" (The colonel's son) introduces Tobías, the son, and Doña Soledad, the mother. The overtones of the Macondo fiction include the mother's name ("Solitude") and a sense of the inevitable destiny present in García Márquez from *Leafstorm* to *Chronicle of a Death Foretold.* For example, the colonel knows exactly when his son will return: "Volverá cuando lo acose el hambre" (360) ("He will return when hunger pursues him"). At the end of the story (or chapter, which is a more appropriate description of this passage), the boy indeed returns home for food.

There are six other "notes" which could be considered rough drafts for later fiction of Macondo. They experiment with narrative techniques, character, and locations. García Márquez uses the child's perspective for the narrator, as in *Leafstorm* in "El Regreso de Meme" (Meme's return). Most of these narrative pieces, however, are written in third-person omniscient point of view, like most of the literature of Macondo. Some of them refer back to the eighteenth and nineteenth centuries, providing background to the family and the situation. The last passage is perhaps the most concentrated effort at synthesizing diverse elements for the creation of a novel. It could be viewed as an important step in the ultimate creation of the unpublished manuscript of the novel *La casa,* and such novels as *Leafstorm* and *One Hundred Years of Soliltude.* This piece focuses on a key element in each of these three novels, the family home itself. Titled "La casa de los Buendía" (The Buendía House), it is not considered a journalistic publication.[12] Colonel Aureliano Buendía returns from a civil war to find his home destroyed. A new home is constructed in the same fashion that much seems to take place in the later Macondo: spontaneously, with no preconceived plan or order. Most of the passage is a description of the home, a successful portrayal of its special qualities, such as its plain severity and its function as part of a venerable family tradition.

A perusal of García Márquez's early journalism is fascinating for several reasons. Foremost of these is the opportunity it affords the reader of his later, truly professional fiction to observe the developments of García Márquez's interests, themes, and narrative techniques. The basic attitudes and world view of the twenty-year-old journalist are amazingly consistent with those of the forty- and fifty-year-old novelist and spokesman for Latin-American intellectuals. The later journalism, logically enough, is similar to both the journalistic writing and certain aspects of the fiction. Neither space nor the relative importance of this journalism within the context of García Márquez's total writing career allows a complete review of this considerable body of writing in its entirety.

A brief review of the journalism written a few years later, after the stay in Europe, shows a writer more concerned with international issues than before. A volume later edited under the title *Cuando era feliz e indocumentado* (When I was happy and undocumented) is a collection of this journalism published originally in 1958 in Caracas.

These articles are witness of a García Márquez impressively knowledgeable about world affairs in general, from the intricacies of Venezuelan politics to the current situation in Cuba and Senegal.

The raucous "El año más famoso del mundo" (The most famous year of the world) is an entertaining overview of world events of the year 1957. He covers the major events in Europe, the United States, Asia, and Latin America. The imaginative juxtaposition of the typical political front-page news with human-interest stories both deflates standard news-story-type journalism and makes for a supremely humorous annual review. He subtitles one section, for example, "Gromyko Moves Up and Brigette Bardot's Neckline Goes Down." He gives the two events equal importance in his report of the year's important events; in fact, he explains Bardot's news first. Similarly, to the news of the Soviet Union's new long-range missile, García Márquez adds the news that the West, more interested in the imminent birth of Gina Lollabrigida's firstborn, paid little notice to the Soviet military gestures. The piece functions on the basis of this constant juxtaposition of the standard political news of supposed major significance with the very human and often equally trivial. García Márquez understands well what most people read with interest most of the time in newspapers.

The remainder of this volume contains pieces much more serious and newslike in tone and context, and others that are much more like fiction. One article, for example, is a report on the present policies with Italian immigrants, and another about a local bishop's work to distribute wealth more equally in Venezuela. A report on the process of obtaining medicine for a dying rabies victim features the best narrative techniques of the suspense thriller. A report on the political situation in Colombia concludes with the perspective of that person who always enjoys a privileged position in García Márquez's writing, the common man in the street.

In recent years García Márquez has published journalism regularly. During the late 1970s and early 1980s he wrote a weekly column for *El Espectador,* the Colombian newspaper that originally sent him to Europe in the mid-1950s as a correspondent. His syndicated columns also appear regularly in much of the Hispanic world. Some of his political positions set forth in these articles, such as his support for Fidel Castro's government in Cuba and his criticism of the policies of the United States, have become more unequivocally delineated than they were before. They are articles covering a broad range of topics that any reader can recognize as having been penned by a master of both standard journalism and innovative fiction.

Chapter Eight
Conclusion

When Gabriel García Márquez was awarded the Nobel Prize for Literature in 1982, it was the most prestigious recognition possible for one of the major writers of the twentieth century. Since his work had already been translated and lauded throughout the world before the decision of the Nobel judges, the Nobel recognition was an effect and not a cause; García Márquez's writing over a period of more than thirty years speaks for itself. Coincidentally, these three decades are marked by a Nobel Prize important to García Márquez's writing at each end of the thirty-year chronology: Faulkner's at the beginning and García Márquez's at the end. In fact, García Márquez published an article in 1950 in which he maintained that the most deserving candidate for the prize was William Faulkner.

Like many contemporary Latin American writers, García Márquez prefers to see his creation as a revolutionary project. Social critic in his fiction and assertively leftist in some of his public ideological positions, García Márquez, nevertheless, is not doctrinaire in his writing. It is more appropriate to compare him with the Nobel Prize winning writer Czeslow Milosz, who has been described as follows: "His reverence for human custom is based on his participation in it." García Márquez's reverence for human custom, and all that is human, is based on a fictional, journalistic, and personal participation in them. García Márquez's ability to capture so much of Hispanic culture and tradition at the same time that he expresses so much of this participation in humanity in a way universally appreciated is one magnificent characteristic of his work. In this sense it is possible to understand García Márquez's own contention that the revolutionary role of the novelist is to "write well."

An overview of this complete writing provides the opportunity for some generalizations. The central core of García Márquez's work, of course, is the fiction of the cycle of Macondo, beginning with *Leafstorm* and culminating in *One Hundred Years of Solitude*. A second cycle, focused above all on the matter of power, includes *The Incredible and Sad Tale of Innocent Eréndira and Her Heartless Grandmother*

and *The Autumn of the Patriarch.* Although it would be difficult to
reach an absolute consensus from critics with respect to García
Márquez's finest novels, most readers would agree that his major
and best written novels are *One Hundred Years of Solitude, The Autumn
of the Patriarch,* and *No One Writes to the Colonel.*

Constant themes and techniques have been analyzed throughout
this study. The presence of death has been noted from the very first
stories to the last novel. The solitude of characters is equally notable
from *Leafstorm* to the latest novel. A fictional world in which predetermined and often inexplicable forces control the actions and
lives of the characters functions concurrently with structures, images, and other narrative techniques that are used similarly throughout García Márquez's fiction. Motivating forces and causes often
eschew rational explanation, both for the characters and the readers.
A corollary to this antirationalist stance is a skepticism of technology
and science. Consequently, the word "progress" does not carry the
same positive overtones for García Márquez that it has enjoyed this
past century in the industrial West.

García Márquez's major contribution to Spanish-American literature, *One Hundred Years of Solitude,* is one of the greatest novels
of the Hispanic tradition since *Don Quixote.* With its publication,
García Márquez both reaffirmed the author's right of invention and
produced one of the finest examples of transcendent regionalism in
the Spanish-American tradition. García Márquez has been quoted
proclaiming, along with the French intellectuals of 1968, "Power
to the Imagination." Although García Márquez was not the only
practitioner of humor in the late 1960s, the publication of *One
Hundred Years of Solitude,* along with Spanish American novels like
Guillermo Cabrera Infante's *Three Trapped Tigers* (1967), marked a
renewed interest in humor in the novel, a characteristic surprisingly
absent before in Spanish-America.

García Márquez's contributions to world literature are both significant and increasing with the passing of time. Although Latin
American writers such as Mario Vargas Llosa, Carlos Fuentes, and
Julio Cortázar have been read outside the Hispanic world, none of
them has a corpus of fiction as accessible as that of García Márquez.
The complex themes, structures, and techniques employed by these
and many other contemporary novelists sometimes limits their readership to a relatively small group. García Márquez's accessibility
has allowed him to showcase both the phenomenal quality of Latin-

American writing and the wonders of Latin-American reality. García Márquez seems to respond to that universal human longing for liberation from the way most contemporary societies have reduced all expression and living to purely rational terms. He has invented a variety of strategies for actively involving the reader in his fictional world, making the process of reading remarkably experiential.

Notes and References

Chapter One

1. Mario Vargas Llosa, "García Márquez: From Aracataca to Macondo," *70 Review* (Center for Inter-American Relations), 1971, 129.
2. Seymour Menton, *La novela colombiana: planetas y satélites* (Bogotá, 1978); Raymond L. Williams, *La novela colombiana contemporánea* (Bogatá: Plaza y Janés, 1976).
3. Raymond L. Williams. *Una década de la novela colombiana: la experiencia de los setenta* (Bogatá, 1981).
4. John S. Brushwood, *The Spanish-American Novel: A Twentieth Century Survey* (Austin, 1975).
5. Personal interview with William Gass, St. Louis, Missouri, April 1982.
6. Harley D. Oberhelman, *The Presence of Faulkner in the Writings of García Márquez* (Lubbock, Tex., 1980), 7.
7. See Brushwood's discussion of the right of invention in the Spanish-American novel in *The Spanish-American Novel,* 157–59.
8. José Donoso, a Chilean contemporary of García Márquez, has explained this situation in *The Boom of the Spanish-American Literature: A Personal History* (New York: Columbia University Press, 1977).
9. John S. Brushwood, "José Felix Fuenmayor y el regionalismo de García Márquez," *Texto Crítico,* no. 7 (May–August 1978):110–15.
10. Ibid., 111.
11. Seymour Menton discusses the latter in *"Respirando el verano:* fuente colombiana de *Cien años de soledad," Revista Iberoamericana,* no. 91 (April–June 1975):203–17.
12. Germán Vargas, "Alvaro Cepeda Samudio," *Golpe de Dados* 8, no. 47 (October 1980):83.
13. Luis Harss and Barbara Dohmann, *Into the Mainstream* (New York, 1967), 319.
14. Gabriel García Márquez, "Fantasía y creación artística en América Latina y el Caribe," *Texto Crítico,* no. 14 (July–September 1979):3–8.
15. Edith Grossman, "Truth Is Stranger Than Fact," *Review,* no. 30 (1981):71–73.
16. Jacques Gilard, "García Márquez, le groupe de Barranquilla, et Faulkner," *Caravelle* no. 27 (1976):161.
17. Oberhelman, *The Presence of Faulkner,* 9.

18. Harss and Dohmann, *Into the Mainstream,* 322.

19. The Sunday literary supplements to newspapers in Colombia, the country's most important literary organs, began to devote considerable attention to Vinyes in the early 1980s. One example is an entire issue of the Sunday supplement of *El Heraldo* (Barranquilla) which is dedicated to Vinyes, 9 May 1982.

20. Harss and Dohmann, *Into the Mainstream,* 317.

21. Mario Vargas Llosa, *Gabriel García Márquez: historia de un deicidio* (Barcelona, 1971), 41.

22. Ibid., 75.

23. Harss and Dohmann, *Into the Mainstream,* 339.

24. Personal interview with García Márquez, October 1975.

Chapter Two

1. George McMurray, for example, does not study these stories in his fine overview of García Márquez's work, *Gabriel García Márquez* (New York, 1977). Mario Vargas Llosa, in his *Historia de un deicidio,* describes them as part of García Márquez's "prehistoria morbosa" ("morbid prehistory").

2. "La tercera resignación," in *Todos los cuentos* (Barcelona, 1975), 10; all quotations in Spanish are from this edition.

3. This story appeared in English in a volume titled *Innocent Erendira and Other Stories* (New York, 1979), 96; all quotations in English for stories in the first section of this chapter are from this edition.

4. Vargas Llosa, *Gabriel García Márquez,* 221.

5. Ibid., 220.

6. Ibid., 228.

7. Ibid., 218.

8. Susan S. Lanser, *The Narrative Act: Point of View in Prose Fiction* (Princeton: Princeton University Press, 1981), 101.

9. The treatment of literature as a symbolic act that attempts to harmonize elements that are ideologically heterogeneous is set forth by Fredric Jameson in *The Political Unconscious: Narrative as a Socially Symbolic Act* (Ithaca: Cornell University Press, 1981); see especially 144.

10. M. Bakhtin defines heteroglossia as such in *The Dialogic Imagination* (Austin: University of Texas Press, 1981), 428.

11. Walter Ong, "The Writer's Audience is Always a Fiction," *PMLA* 90, no. 1 (January 1975):9–21.

12. "Invierno" ("Winter") is a common euphemism for rain in Colombia.

13. Gabriel García Márquez, *Leafstorm and Other Stories* (New York, 1973), 197; all quotations in English are from this edition.

14. Vargas Llosa, *Gabriel García Márquez,* 239.

15. *Relato de un náufrago* (Bogotá, 1979), 48; all quotations in Spanish are from this edition.
16. See García Márquez's introduction to the story in his "La historia de mi historia," in *Relato de un náufrago*, 9.
17. Jameson, *The Political Unconscious*, 87.
18. Vargas Llosa, *Gabriel García Márquez*, 246.
19. Ibid., 233.
20. *Leafstorm and Other Stories*, 24.
21. *El olor de la guayaba* (Bogotá, 1982), 58; the translation into English is mine.
22. Ibid.
23. Brushwood, *The Spanish American Novel*, 200.
24. Robert L. Sims, "Theme, Narrative *Bricolage* and Myth in García Márquez," *Journal of Spanish Studies: Twentieth Century* 8, no. 12 (Spring—Fall 1980):143–57.
25. Ibid., 75.
26. Brushwood, *The Spanish American Novel*, 334–35.
27. *La hojarasca* (Bogotá, 1974), 46.
28. McMurray, *Gabriel García Márquez*, 17.

Chapter Three

1. Charles Bergquist discusses this aspect of the Caribbean coast in an article still unpublished at the time of this writing: "Gabriel García Márquez: A Colombian Anomaly." This paper was presented at the Conference on Literature and History in Twentieth Century Latin America, Washington University in St. Louis, 13–15 April 1983.
2. Brushwood discusses the work of Osorio Lizarazo, Caballero Calderón, and Zapata Olivella in *The Spanish American Novel*. See pp. 84, 117, 149, and 264 for analysis of Osorio Lizarazo; pp. 180, 189–90, and 270–71 for analysis of Caballero Calderón; pp. 227–28 and 282–83 for analysis of Zapata Olivella.
3. García Márquez made this statement in an interview with E. González Bermejo, "Ahora 200 años de soledad," *Oiga*, no. 392 (September 1970):31.
4. *El olor de la guayaba*, 60.
5. *Los funerales de la Mamá Grande* (Buenos Aires, 1974), 127. All the stories discussed in this chapter are from this edition. The remainder of the stories discussed in section 2 of this chapter are from this edition.
6. *No One Writes to the Colonel and Other Stories* (New York, 1979), 153. The remainder of the stories discussed in sections 2–3 of this chapter are from this edition.
7. This concept of the nuclear verb is from Gérard Genette's "Discours du récit," in *Figures III* (Paris: Seuil, 1972). In the introduction

Genette sets forth the possibility of considering a story on the basis of the expansion of a verb. For example, Genette notes that in the *Odyssey* the verb would be "Ulysses returns to Ithaca" and in *A la Recherche du temps perdu* "Marcel becomes a writer."

8. Sims, "Theme," 147.

9. Ibid., 144.

10. David William Foster, "The Double Inscription of the *Narrataire* 'Los funerales de la Mamá Grande,' " in *Studies in the Contemporary Spanish-American Short Story* (Columbia, 1979),51–62.

11. Ibid., 52–53.

12. Ibid., 53.

13. Ibid., 39–50.

14. Ibid., 40.

15. Regina Janes mentions the similarities with Hemingway in *Gabriel García Márquez: Revolutions in Wonderland* (Columbia, 1981), see p. 35.

16. Ángel Rama, "Un novelista de la violencia americana," in *Nueve asedios a García Márquez* (Santiago: Editorial Universitaria, 1969), 118–19.

17. Vargas Llosa, *Gabirel García Márquez,* 317.

18. *El coronel no tiene quien le escriba* (Bogotá, 1975), 9.

19. Colombia has been in an officially declared "Estado de Sitio" or "State of Siege" during much of the twentieth century.

20. McMurray, *Gabriel García Márquez,* 27.

21. Janes, *Gabriel García Márquez,* 34.

22. Wolfgang A. Luchting, "¿Quién escribe los pasquines?" *El Café Literario* 5, nos. 29–30 (September–December 1982):13–19.

23. *La mala hora* (Buenos Aires, Editorial Sudamericana, 1974), 100–1.

24. *In Evil Hour* (New York, 1979), 88.

25. McMurray, *Gabriel García Márquez,* 41.

26. Bakhtin, *The Dialogic Imagination,* 428.

Chapter Four

1. *El olor de la guayaba,* 75.

2. Brushwood, *The Spanish-American Novel,* 287–88.

3. Red is the traditional color of the Liberal party in Colombia. Blue is associated with the Conservatives. Houses and even entire towns are often painted these colors to demonstrate party affiliation.

4. *Cien años de soledad* (Buenos Aires, 1970), 88.

5. *One Hundred Years of Solitude* (New York, 1971), 97.

6. See Brushwood, *The Spanish-American Novel,* 287–88, and Seymour Menton, *"One Hundred Years of Solitude,"* an unpublished lecture

presented in the Distinguished Faculty Lecture series, University of California, Irvine, 24 January 1980.

7. McMurray discusses the ending of the novel in *Gabriel García Márquez*, 85.

8. Angel Flores, "Magical Realism in Spanish American Fiction," *Hispania* 38 (1955):187–92.

9. McMurray, *Gabriel García Márquez*, 165.

10. Miguel Fernández-Braso, *La soledad de Gabriel García Márquez* (Barcelona: Planeta, 1972), 86.

11. E. González Bermejo, "Ahora 200 años de soledad," *Oiga*, no. 392 (September 1970):31.

12. Sims, "Theme," 154.

13. For a reading based on psychology and archetype, see Josefina Ludmer, *Cien años de soledad: una interpretación* (Buenos Aires, 1972).

14. Suzanne Jill Levine provides an overview of the literary antecedents in *El espejo hablado* (Caracas, 1975).

15. Ibid., 46–54.

16. See Oberhelman, *The Presence of Faulkner*.

17. Lucila Inés Mena provides an overview of history and this novel in *La función de la historia en Cien años de soledad* (Barcelona, 1979). See especially chapter 1.

18. Mena reviews similarities between Uribe and Buendía in ibid., 47–62.

19. Charles Bergquist, "Gabriel García Márquez: A Colombian Anomaly" (unpublished paper).

20. *El olor de la guayaba*, 77.

21. Bakhtin, *The Dialogic Imagination*, 428.

22. Julio Ortega, "Cien años de soledad," in *La contemplación y la fiesta* (Caracas, 1969), 117–33.

23. Wayne Booth, *The Rhetoric of Fiction* (Chicago: University of Chicago Press, 1961), 125.

Chapter Five

1. I have studied the "phenomenon of Macondo" in more detail in a book published in Spanish, *Una década de la novela colombiana: la experiencia de los setenta*. See especially chapter 7.

2. This reading experience of the original volume is not yet available in English. In the original Spanish edition, the stories in this volume appear in the following order: "A Very Old Man with Enormous Wings," "The Sea of Lost Time," "The Handsomest Drowned Man in the World," "Death Constant Beyond Love," "The Last Voyage of the Ghost Ship," "Blacaman the Good, Vendor of Miracles," and "The Incredible and Sad Tale of Innocent Eréndira and Her Heartless Grandmother."

3. *La increíble y triste historia de la cándida Eréndira y de su abuela desalmada* (Barcelona, 1972), 20.

4. *Leafstorm and Other Stories,* 167.

5. Vargas Llosa explains that they were originally written as children's tales in his *Gabriel García Márquez,* 617. In the English edition, "A Very Old Man with Enormous Wings" and "The Handsomest Drowned Man in the World" carry the subtitle "A Tale for Children."

6. See Janes, *Gabriel García Márquez,* 79.

7. *Leafstorm and Other Stories,* 171.

8. The stories which appear in the English edition of *Innocent Eréndira and Other Stories* are not the same ones that appeared in the original Spanish volume with the same title story. The English edition includes the title story and two stories from the original Spanish edition, "The Sea of Lost Time" and "Death Constant Beyond Love." The remaining nine stories in this English edition were originally published in Spanish from 1948 to 1952, García Márquez's first published stories.

9. *Innocent Eréndira and Other Stories* (New York, 1979), 7.

10. *Innocent Eréndira and Other Stories,* 187.

11. Janes makes this point in *Gabriel García Márquez,* 81.

Chapter Six

1. *El olor de la guayaba,* 88.

2. Ibid., 86.

3. Ibid., 85.

4. Ibid., 89.

5. *The Autumn of the Patriarch* (New York, 1977), p. 119; all quotations in English are from this edition.

6. This reference to Gérard Genette is explained in "Discours du récit" which appears in *Figures III* (Paris: Sevil, 1972). In the introduction Genette suggests the possibility of considering a story on the basis of the expansion of a verb. He notes that for the *Odyssey* the verb would be "Ulysses returns to Ithaca" and for *A la Recherche du temps perdu,* "Marcel becomes a writer."

7. This structure was originally delineated in my article "The Dynamic Structure of García Márquez's *El otoño del patriarca,*" *Symposium* 32, no. 1 (Spring 1978):56–75. The analysis in this article contains more textual references than the length of this chapter allows.

8. *El otoño del patriarca* (Buenos Aires, 1975), 8; all quotations in Spanish are from this edition.

9. José Miguel Oviedo has noted the progression in sentence length. See "García Márquez: la novela como taumaturgia," *American Hispanist* 1, no. 2 (October 1975): 7.

10. *El olor de la guayaba,* 87.

11. John M. Lipski discusses the changes in narrative perspective in "Embedded Dialogue in *El otoño del patriarca,*" *American Hispanist* 2, no. 14 (January 1977):9–12.

12. Julio Ortega discusses the implications of impersonal expressions such as "se sabía" in *"El otoño del patriarca:* texto y cultura," *Hispanic Review* 46 (1978):421–46.

13. George McMurray discusses the characterization of the General as a myth in *Gabriel García Márquez,* pp. 129–56.

14. Seymour Menton has suggested that even what is seen cannot be believed. Yet only that which is seen offers the possibility of being believed. See "Ver para no creer: *El otoño del patriarca,*" *Caribe* 1, no. 1 (Spring 1976):7–27.

Chapter Seven

1. See Edith Grossman, "The Truth Is Stranger Than Fact," *Review,* no. 30 (September–December 1981):71–73.

2. Ibid., 72.

3. *Chronicle of a Death Foretold* (New York, 1983), 3; All quotations are from this edition.

4. Julio Roca and Camilo Calderón, *Al Día* (Bogotá), no. 1 (28 April 1981):51–60, 108–9.

5. José Miguel Oviedo points this out in "Gabriel García Márquez: A la (Mala) Hora Señalada" (unpublished).

6. Jameson, *The Political Unconscious,* 428.

7. Oviedo, "Gabriel García Márquez."

8. William Gass, review of *Chronicle of a Death Foretold, New York,* 11 April 1983, 83.

9. Daniel Samper Pizano, "Crónica sobre un destino anunciado," *Lecturas Dominicales, El Tiempo,* 18 June 1981, 8–10.

10. See Germán Carrillo, *"Crónica de una muerte anunciada* de G. García Márquez: reportaje, profecía y recuento," in *Literatures in Transition: The Many Voices of the Caribbean Area* (Gaithersburg: Hispamérica, 1983), 77–83.

11. *Textos costeños,* with prologue by Jacques Gilard (Barcelona, 1981), 242; further quotations from García Márquez's journalism during the 1948–52 period are from this volume.

12. Jacques Gilard includes these pieces in an appendice to the *Textos costeños,* explained on p. 877.

Selected Bibliography

PRIMARY SOURCES

1. Spanish Editions

La hojarasca. Bogotá: Ediciones Sipa, 1955.

El coronel no tiene quien le escriba. Medellín, Colombia: Aguirre Editor, 1961.

Los funerales de la Mamá Grande. Xalapa, Mexico: Editorial Universidad Veracruzana, 1962. Contains "La siesta del martes," "Un día de estos," "En este pueblo no hay ladrones," "La prodigiosa tarde de Baltazar," "La viuda de Montiel," "Un día después del sábado," "Rosas artificiales," and "Los funerales de la Mamá Grande."

La mala hora. Madrid: Talleres de Gráficas Luis Pérez, 1962.

Cien años de soledad. Buenos Aires: Editorial Sudamericana, 1967.

Isabel viendo llover en Macondo. Buenos Aires: Editorial Estuario, 1967.

La novela en América Latina: Diálogo. Lima: Carlos Milla Batres, 1968. With Mario Vargas Llosa.

Relato de un náufrago. Barcelona: Tusquets Editor, 1970.

La increíble y triste historia de la cándida Eréndira y de su abuela desalmada. Barcelona: Barral Editores, 1972. Contains "Un señor muy viejo con unas alas enormes," "El mar del tiempo perdido," "El ahogado más hermoso del mundo," "Muerte constante más allá del amor," "El último viaje del buque fantasma," "Blacamán el bueno vendedor de milagros," and "La increíble y triste historia de la cándida Eréndira y de su abuela desalmada."

El negro que hizo esperar a los ángeles. Montevideo: Ediciones Alfil, 1972. Contains "Nabo, el negro que hizo esperar a los ángeles," "Alguien desordena estas rosas," "La mujer que llegaba a las seis," "Ojos de perro azul," "Diálogo del espejo," "Amargura para tres sonámbulos," "Eva está dentro de su gato," "La otra costilla de la muerte," and "La tercera resignación."

Ojos de perro azul. Rosario, Argentina: Equiseditorial, 1972. Contains "La tercera resignación," "La otra costilla de la muerte," "Eva está dentro de su gato," "Amargura para tres sonámbulos," "Diálogo del espejo," "Ojos de perro azul," "La mujer que llegaba a las seis," "Nabo, el negro que hizo esperar a los ángeles," "Alguien desordena estas rosas,"

"La noche de los alcaravanes," and "Monólogo de Isabel viendo llover en Macondo."

Cuando era feliz e indocumentado. Caracas: Ediciones El Ojo del Camello, 1973.

Cuatro cuentos. Mexico City: Comunidad Latinoamérica de Escritores, 1974.

El otoño del patriarca. Barcelona: Plaza y Janés, 1975.

Todos los cuentos de Gabriel García Márquez (1947–1972). Barcelona: Plaza y Janés, 1975.

Crónicas y reportajes. Bogotá: Instituto Colombiano de Cultura, 1976.

Operación Carlota. Lima: Mosca Azuel, 1977.

Periodismo militante. Bogotá: Son de máquina Editores, 1978.

Obra periodística. 3 vols. Barcelona: Bruguera, 1982.

2. English Translations

No One Writes to the Colonel and Other Stories. Translated by J. S. Bernstein. New York: Harper & Row, 1968. Contains "No One Writes to the Colonel," "Tuesday Siesta," "One of These Days," "There Are No Thieves in This Town," "Baltazar's Marvelous Afternoon," "Montiel's Widow," "One Day After Saturday," "Artificial Roses," and "Big Mama's Funeral."

One Hundred Years of Solitude. Translated by Gregory Rabassa. New York: Harper & Row, 1970.

Leafstorm and Other Stories. Translated by Gregory Rabassa. New York: Harper & Row, 1972. Contains "Leafstorm," "The Handsomest Drowned Man in the World," "A Very Old Man With Enormous Wings," "Blacamán the Good, Vendor of Miracles," "The Last Voyage of the Ghost Ship," "Monologue of Isabel Watching It Rain in Macondo," and "Nabo."

The Autumn of the Patriarch. Translated by Gregory Rabassa. New York: Harper & Row, 1976.

In Evil Hour. New York: Avon Bard, 1979.

Innocent Eréndira and Other Stories. New York: Harper Colophon Books, 1979. Contains "The Incredible and Sad Tale of Innocent Eréndira and Her Heartless Grandmother," "The Sea of Lost Time," "Death Constant Beyond Love," "The Third Resignation," "The Other Side of Death," "Eva is Inside Her Cat," "Dialogue with the Mirror," "Bitterness for Three Sleepwalkers," "Eyes for a Blue Dog," "The Woman Who Came at Six O'Clock," "Someone Has Been Disarranging These Roses," and "The Night of the Curlews."

Chronicle of a Death Foretold. New York: Alfred A. Knopf, 1982.

The Fragrance of the Guava: Plinio Apuleyo Mendoza in conversation with Gabriel García Márquez. London: Verso, 1983.

SECONDARY SOURCES

1. Books

Benedetti, Mario et al. *Nueve asedios a García Márquez*. Santiago, Chile: Editorial Universitaria, 1971. A collection of critical essays by distinguished scholars of Latin American literature.

Brushwood, John S. *The Spanish-American Novel: A Twentieth Century Survey*. Austin: University of Texas Press, 1975. The most complete analytical study available on the Spanish-American novel of the twentieth century. It includes commentary on Colombian novels of the twentieth century and analysis of each of García Márquez's novels of the 1950s and 1960s.

Carrillo, Germán. *La narrativa de Gabriel Garía Márquez*. Madrid: Ediciones de Arte y Bibliografía, 1975. Interpretive essays on *One Hundred Years of Solitude* and many of the short stories.

Fau, Margaret Eustella. *Gabriel García Márquez: An Annotated Bibliography, 1947–1979*. Westport, Conn.: Greenwood Press, 1980. The most complete bibliography available.

Fuenmayor, Alfonso. *Crónicas sobre el Grupo de Barranquilla*. Bogotá: Instituto Colombiano de Cultura, 1978. Brief journalistic accounts on the literary and cultural activities of the Group of Barranquilla during the late 1940s and 1950s.

González del Valle, Luis, and Cabrera, Vicente. *La nueva ficción hispanoamericana a través de Miguel Angel Asturias y Gabriel García Márquez*. New York: Eliseo Torres, 1972. Includes four essays on the work of García Márquez.

Gullón, Ricardo. *García Márquez o el olvidado arte de contar*. Madrid: Taurus, 1970. An analysis of narrative techniques in *One Hundred Years of Solitude*.

Harss, Luis, and Dohmann, Barbara. *Into the Mainstream*. New York: Harper & Row, 1967. A combination of interviews and intelligent readings of novels. This book provides valuable insights into the writing of major Latin American writers, including García Márquez.

Janes, Regina. *Gabriel García Márquez: Revolutions in Wonderland*. Columbia: University of Missouri Press, 1981. Brief but perceptive readings of García Márquez's major fiction.

Jara Cuadra, René, and Mejía Duque, Jaime. *Las claves del mito en García Márquez*. Valparaíso, Chile: Ediciones Universitarias, 1972. A study of myth as a key to an understanding of the fiction of García Márquez.

Levine, Suzanne Jill. *El espejo hablado*. Caracas: Monte Avila, 1975. Well-researched study which places García Márquez's writing within the context of world literature, demonstrating the influence of writers such as Virginia Woolf and Borges.

Lorenz, Günter. *Dialog mit Lateinamerika.* Tübingen: Horst Edmann Verlag, 1970. A useful set of interviews with major Latin American writers, including García Márquez.

Ludmer, Josefina. *Cien años de soledad: una interpretación.* Buenos Aires: Tiempo Contemporáneo, 1972. A provocative and exceptionally insightful reading of *One Hundred Years of Solitude,* based primarily on concepts of structuralist and neo-Freudian theorists.

McMurray, George. *Gabriel García Márquez.* New York: Frederick Ungar, 1977. This study offers sound and perceptive readings of García Márquez's major fiction.

Mena, Lucila Inés. *La función de la historia en Cien años de soledad.* Barcelona: Plaza y Janés, 1979. Provides the historical background to *One Hundred Years of Solitude.*

Menton, Seymour. *La novela colombiana: planetas y satélites.* Bogotá: Plaza y Janés, 1978. A carefully researched book which offers analysis of major Colombian novels from *María* (1867) to the present. Includes a chapter on *The Autumn of the Patriarch.*

Oberhelman, Harley D. *The Presence of Faulkner in the Writings of García Márquez.* Lubbock, Tex.: Texas Tech Press, 1980. A valuable and well-documented study on the influence of Faulkner on García Márquez.

Vargas Llosa, Mario. *Gabriel García Márquez: historia de un deicidio.* Barcelona: Barral; Carácas: Monte Avila, 1971. An authoritative and exhaustive study on the complete work of García Márquez published by 1970. Contains the most informative biography available.

Williams, Raymond L. *Una década de la novela colombiana: la experiencia de los setenta.* Bogotá: Plaza y Janés, 1981. Analysis of the major Colombian novels of the 1970s, including *The Autumn of the Patriarch.*

2. Articles

Balladares Cuadra, José Emilio. *"Cien años de soledad:* de la vida y máscara de la muerte de la América Hispana." *Revista del pensamiento centroamericano* (Managua), 31, no. 152 (July–September 1976): 1–60. Outstanding reading of *One Hundred Years of Solitude,* divided into four parts: (1) the matron of Ephesus: orthogenesis of a story, (2) orthogenesis of a culture, (3) heterogenous influences, and (4) *One Hundred Years of Solitude:* an interpretation.

Benedetti, Mario. "El recurso del supremo patriarca." *Casa de las Américas* 17, no. 98 (September–October 1976):12–23. Focuses on the role of the dictator in *The Autumn of the Patriarch.*

Bergquist, Charles. "Gabriel García Márquez: A Colombian Anomaly." Paper presented at Conference on Literature and History in Twentieth

Century Latin America, Washington University in St. Louis, 13–15 April 1983. Historical and economic background to Colombia which argues convincingly that García Márquez's literary production is a result of the special historical and economic conditions of the Caribbean coastal region. Bergquist is an historian.

Brushwood, John S. "José Féliz Fuenmayor y el regionalismo de García Márquez." *Texto crítico* 3, No. 7 (May–August 1977):110–15. Demonstrates that García Márquez forms part of a unique coastal tradition of Faulknerian writing.

Ciplijauskaité, Birute. "Foreshadowing as a Technique and Theme in *One Hundred Years of Solitude*." *Books Abroad* 47, no. 3 (1973):479–84. A detailed analysis of the use of the technique of foreshadowing in *One Hundred Years of Solitude*.

Foster, David William. "The Double Inscription of the *Narrataire* in 'Los funerales de la Mamá Grande.' " In *Studies in the Contemporary Spanish American Short Story*. Columbia: University of Missouri Press, 1979, 51–62. A type of reading new to many Hispanists, using concepts of recent literary theory. An incisive analysis of the reader in García Márquez.

————. "García Márquez and the *Écriture* of Complicity: 'La prodigiosa tarde de Baltazar.' " In *Studies in the Contemporary Spanish American Short Story*, 39–50. An approach similar to the one described above.

————. "García Márquez and Solitude." *Americas*, no. 21 (November–December 1969):36–41. A study of the theme of solitude in *One Hundred Years of Solitude*, within the context of biblical tradition.

Franco, Jean. "The Limits of Liberal Imagination: *One Hundred Years of Solitude* and *Nostromo*." *Punto de contacto/Point of Contact* 1, no. 1 (December 1975):4–16. A well-conceived ideological analysis of *One Hundred Years of Solitude*.

————. "Gabriel García Márquez," in *An Introduction to Spanish American Literature*. Cambridge: Cambridge Press, 1969, 343–47. Presents García Márquez's major themes and an analysis of *One Hundred Years of Solitude*.

Fuentes, Carlos. "Gabriel García Márquez: la segunda lectura," in *La nueva novela hispanoamericana*. Mexico City: Joaquín Mortiz, 1969, 58–67. A profound study of *One Hundred Years of Solitude*, noting the tensions between utopia, time, and myth.

Gilard, Jacques. "García Márquez, le groupe de Barranquilla, et Faulkner." *Caravelle* 27 (1976):123–46. Investigative study of García Márquez's early readings and writings.

González Echevarría, Roberto. "The Dictatorship of Rhetoric/The Rhetoric of Dictatorship: Carpentier, García Márquez and Roa Bastos." *Latin American Research Review* 15, no. 3 (1980):205–28. Contains brief commentary on *The Autumn of the Patriarch,* offering a reading in light of recent ideas of the poststructuralist theorist Jacques Derrida.

Kadir, Djelal. "The Architectonic Principle of *Cien años de soledad* and the Vichian Theory of History." *Kentucky Romance Quarterly* 24, no. 3 (1977):251–61. A thought-provoking analysis of history in *One Hundred Years of Solitude,* using Vico's theories of history as a point of departure.

Kirsner, Robert. "Four Colombian Novels of Violence." *Hispania* 49, no. 1 (March 1966):70–74. A sociological study of four Colombian novels, including García Márquez's *Leafstorm.*

Levy, Kurt. "Planes of Reality in *El otoño del patriarca.*" In *Studies in Honor of Gerald E. Wade.* Madrid, 1979, 133–41. Commentary on major themes and techniques in *The Autumn of the Patriarch.*

Luchting, Wolfgang A. "Gabriel García Márquez: The Boom and the Whimper." *Books Abroad* 44, no. 1 (Winter 1970):26–30. A discussion of *One Hundred Years of Solitude* as a model for Latin American literature today.

———. "¿Quién escribe los pasquines?" *El café literario,* 5, nos. 29–30 (September–December 1982):13–19. A provocative reading of *In Evil Hour,* which proposes that the lampoons in the novel are a metaphor for fiction.

McGrady, Donald. "Acerca de una colección desconocida de relatos por Gabriel García Márquez." *Thesuarus* 27, no. 2 (May–August 1972):293–320. One of the few studies of the early stories published from 1948 to 1954.

Muller-Bergh, Klaus. "*Relato de un náufrago:* García Márquez's Tale of Shipwreck and Survival at Sea." *Books Abroad* 47, no. 3 (1973):460–66. A valuable introductory study to "A Tale of a Castaway."

Oberhelman, Harley Dean. "García Márquez and the American South." *Chasqui* 5, no. 1 (November 1975):29–38. A study which demonstrates the influence of Faulkner in García Márquez's writing and draws parallels between the American South and Colombia.

Ortega, Julio. "*Cien años de soledad.*" In *La contemplación y la fiesta.* Caracas: Monte Avila, 1969, 117–33. A valuable reading of *One Hundred Years of Solitude,* emphasizing archetypes.

———. "*El otoño del patriarca:* texto y cultura." *Hispanic Review* 46 (1978):421–46. Commentary on culture, myth, and codes in *The Autumn of the Patriarch,* written by a critic well versed in structuralism and semiotics.

Oviedo, José Miguel. "García Márquez: la novela como taumaturgia." *The American Hispanist* 1, no. 2 (October 1975):7–9. Superb introductory analysis of *The Autumn of the Patriarch.*

Rama, Angel. "Un patriarca en la remozada galería de dictadores." *Eco* 29, no. 178 (August 1975):408–43. A consideration of the figure of the dictator in *Leafstorm, One Hundred Years of Solitude* and *The Autumn of the Patriarch.*

Rodríguez Monegal, Emir. *"One Hundred Years of Solitude:* The Last Three Pages." *Books Abroad* 47, no. 3 (1973):485–89. An analysis of the last three pages of *One Hundred Years of Solitude,* revealing their importance to the total novel.

Salgado, María. "Civilización y barbarie o imaginación y barbarie." *Explicación de textos literarios* 4, supp. 1 (1976):299–312. A study of García Márquez's use of the classic Latin American theme of civilization vs. barbarity in *One Hundred Years of Solitude.*

Segre, Cesare. "Il tempo curvo di García Márquez." *I signi e la critica,* January 1969, 251–95. A thorough analysis of time and its effects in *One Hundred Years of Solitude.*

Siemens, William. "Tiempo, entropia y la estructura de *Cien años de soledad." Explicación de Textos Literarios* 4, no. 1 (1976):359–71. A study which demonstrates how the past, present, and future are fused in *One Hundred Years of Solitude.*

Sims, Robert L. "Theme, Narrative Bricolage and Myth in García Márquez." *Journal of Spanish Studies: Twentieth Century* 8, nos. 1–2 (Spring–Fall 1980):145–59. Provides valuable insights into the development of myth from García Márquez's early fiction to *One Hundred Years of Solitude.*

Vargas, Germán. "Alvaro Cepeda Samudio." *Golpe de dados,* 8, no. 48 (October 1980):4–16. One of the most informative pieces available on the "Group of Barranquilla," written by one of the members of the group.

————. "Un personaje: Aracataca." In *Recopilación de textos sobre García Márquez.* Havana: Casa de las Américas, 1969, 139–42. Demonstrates how *One Hundred Years of Solitude* is a composite of themes, characters and situations of previous works.

Williams, Raymond L. "Los comienzos de un Premio Nobel: La tercera resignación." *El café literario* 5, nos. 29–30 (September–December 1982):39–41. An analysis of García Márquez's first story, viewed within the context of his later fiction.

————. "The Dynamic Structure of García Márquez's *El otoño del patriarca." Symposium* 32, no. 1 (Spring 1978):56–75. Close reading of *The Autumn of the Patriarch,* dealing with the novel's structure.

Index